C000230652

Hill W
Atlantic

34 One-day Walking Routes on the Western Seaboard

DAVID HERMAN

SHANKSMARE PUBLICATIONS

.... 'for be it remembered that to him alone who travels on Shank's mare do the mountains reveal their beauties and their wonders'

From '*Moonbeams*' by John Herman Rice (1917)

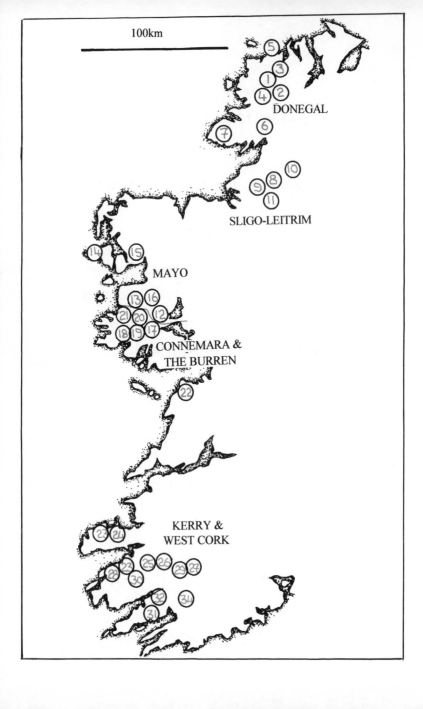

100km

5
3
1
2
4
DONEGAL
6
7

10
8
9
11
SLIGO-LEITRIM

14
15
MAYO

13 16
21 20 12
18 19 17
CONNEMARA &
THE BURREN

22

KERRY &
WEST CORK

23 24

23
28 25 26 29 27
30
32 34
31

CONTENTS

Introduction; The Mountains of Atlantic Ireland; How to Use this Book; Getting to Atlantic Ireland; Getting Around Atlantic Ireland; Accommodation; Maps; Safety; What to Carry with You; Rights of Way and Good Conduct; They're your Mountains too - Get Involved!; Useful Contacts.

DONEGAL

1   Errigal from the North
2   Dooish
3   The Aghlas
4   Slieve Snaght
5   Horn Head
6   Bluestacks
7   Slieve League

SLIGO-LEITRIM

8   The Glencar Escarpment
9   Castlegal
10   Eagle Rock
11   The Doons and Leean

MAYO

12   Bunnacunneen
13   Mweelrea
14   Croaghaun (Achill)
15   Glendahurk (Nephins)
16   Ben Gorm

CONNEMARA & THE BURREN

17   Gleninagh Circuit
18   The Benlettery Horseshoe
19   The Failmore Circuit
20   The Northern Maumturks
21   The Benchoonas
22   The Burren

KERRY & WEST CORK

23   Brandon
24   Circuit of Glanteenassig
25   The Beenkeragh Ridge
26   The Reeks Ridge
27   Bennaunmore
28   Knocknadobar
29   Mangerton
30   Mullaghanattin
31   Hungry Hill
32   Cummeengeera
33   Coomasaharn
34   Gougane Barra

INTRODUCTION

This book covers the mountains facing the Atlantic Ocean on the west coast of Ireland. The routes described are mostly a distillation of the most popular and enjoyable routes in the previously published books named on the inside front cover. Though I have walked the entire length of some of the routes since the publication of these books, I confess that I have not walked every inch of every route since then. However, I have looked at the beginning and end of nearly every route, the sections where changes are most likely to occur. I have also enquired about changes which may have occurred at other points on each route, so I am reasonably satisfied that the routes are up to date.

To walk the routes in this book Ordnance Survey (OS) maps are not absolutely necessary as the black and white extracts from these maps given here should be enough to get you safely round the route. There is more about this below.

This book covers a large area including most of the best hill walking country in Ireland, so a choice of routes was quite difficult. I have attempted to give as representative a selection of walks as possible, consistent with the overall aim of offering what are the best (only one person's opinion!). Where possible - and it hasn't always been possible - one or more shorter variations of each main route are given so that if you do not wish to do the harder walk or if weather conditions are unfavourable you will at least have the opportunity of walking a route that gives you some idea of the area.

THE MOUNTAINS OF ATLANTIC IRELAND

Let's start in the north-west and work our way down the coast looking briefly at the mountain ranges in turn.

The mountains of **Donegal** offer much varied walking. In the very north there are some good coastal walks (route 5). Further south the parallel lines of mountains (routes 1-4) makes looped walks a little difficult to devise. Here Errigal (751m) is the best known peak and the great dome of Slieve Snaght (678m) possibly the most impressive. South of these ranges is an undistinguished moorland, but just north of Donegal town is the fascinating granite slab country of the Bluestacks (674m) (route 6), a much underrated area, perhaps because it has no definite peaks. To the west of the Bluestacks is the great westward-thrusting bulge of Rossaun, where Slieve League (595m) (route 7) provides one of several excellent cliff walks.

South of Donegal and to the east of the large town of Sligo are the easily accessible plateaus of **Sligo and Leitrim**. Benbulben (526m) is the best-known mountain here, a boggy plateau bounded by a great sweep of riven cliff. This basic topography is repeated in the several plateaus in the area: a rim of cliff enlivened by the occasional gully and weird rock formation, surrounding a comparatively tame plateau (routes 8-11).

Mayo has several ranges of mountains, not all in the first rank. Achill Island (688m), connected to the mainland by a bridge, has a lovely sea-cliff walk at its remote western end (route 14). More accessible are the Nephins, where the main range rises to 716m (route 15). Though large, much of it is dull and gently sloping with only a few memorable circuits. The Bunnacunneens are similar to the Nephins but smaller (route 12). The Mweelrea area (814m) (route 13) is undoubtedly the high point (both senses) in the county: a group of several high peaks guarded by imposing corries, with small but impressive ranges directly to its east (route 16). Croagh Patrick has a magnificent location south of Clew Bay; with some reluctance I have omitted it because of its dreadful pilgrimage track.

Neighbouring **Connemara** to the south is dominated by the Twelve Bens (729m) and the Maumturks (702m). Both are small but rocky and demanding ranges and infinitely rewarding. The Twelve Bens (routes 17, 18) are the better; indeed, many would say that with their tight, demanding circuits and steep slopes, they are the best walking range in the country. The Maumturks (routes 19, 20) suffer by having a linear layout and far less imposing peaks; nonetheless this is a fine range. The tiny Benchoonas (598m) (route 21) to the north of the Bens cannot offer long walks but is a lovely, undemanding range.

Lumped in with Connemara in this book, though only because of physical proximity and not similar geology (which is unique) is the **Burren** (route 22). It rises to only 344m, but its limestone slabs and fascinating flora make it well worth a short visit for even the most dedicated hill walker.

Lastly **Kerry and West Cork** in the south-west. This area boasts the highest ranges in the country (including all of the few mountains over 1000m) piled up on long rocky peninsulas.

In the north is the *Dingle* peninsula (routes 23, 24), where the remote but magnificent Brandon (952m), with its long line of cliffs and corries, is the most memorable area.

Southwards is the large peninsula of *Iveragh*, which boasts a whole tangle of mighty mountains. The most notable of these are the Reeks (routes 25, 26), which rise to 1039m at Carrauntoohil, the highest of many high and impressive peaks in this area. However the whole peninsula from low but rugged Bennaunmore (454m) (route 27) westward over the corries of Mangerton (839m) (route 29), the striking pyramid of Mullaghanattin (773m) (route 30) to the ocean at Coomasaharn and Knocknadobar (690m) (routes 33, 28) is a marvellous area to explore.

Farther south again is the smaller *Beara* peninsula, more remote and less visited than the others, which contains some memorable circuits and mountains of which Cummeengeera (route 32) and Hungry Hill (685m) (route 31), the latter guarded by mighty cliffs and stern slabs, are the best known. Directly inland of the Iveragh and Beara peninsulas the mountains are generally less rugged but nonetheless cover some good walking country (route 34).

HOW TO USE THIS BOOK

The following notes refer to each of the headings which make up each route description.

'Getting There': The letters 'GR' used under this heading (and occasionally elsewhere) stand for 'grid reference' and the four- or six-digit number following uniquely identifies a point on the map. The system is explained on all OS maps.

To get to the starting point of many of these routes involves miles of travel on bad minor, and nearly as bad (supposedly) major roads. To add to your difficulties you will find that the signposting off the main (N) roads is execrable, and worse than useless in that some signs have been rotated to point the wrong way (oh, the delicious sense of humour of some of my countrymen!). With this in mind it may be worthwhile to pay particular attention to the tedious details of how to get to the start of each route. Otherwise you may find that you are lost before you even get out of your car!

There is information about using bus services below.

'Walking Time': This time is based on a variation of Naismith's Rule. It allows one hour for 4km on the flat plus one hour for each 500m of climbing. Thus a walk of 2km on the flat with a climb of 250m should take 1 hour. This is a fairly leisurely pace but it does not allow time for eating, taking photographs or any other normal stops. Where justified this walking time is adjusted for difficult terrain (eg steep descents, rough vegetation) or easy terrain (eg good tracks).

'Difficulties': This is mostly self-explanatory, but note that wet ground can make routes much more difficult, especially routes that involve scrambling or clambering over rocks. Heavy rain might make streams which are normally fordable completely impassable.

'Map': gives the best map(s) for the route. This is generally the appropriate 1:50 000 OS Discovery Series sheet for which the sheet number only is given. You do not need these maps unless you think you might wander off the black-and-white extract given with the route description. Unless absolutely necessary, no attempt has been made to correct errors on the map extracts, but these errors are referred to in the text. There is more about OS maps below.

Don't forget that you must add the magnetic deviation to the grid bearing to obtain the compass bearing. The deviation varies from 7° in the north to 6° in the south.

'Route': The place names used in this paragraph (and of course elsewhere) are those used on the OS Discovery Series maps regardless of whether they are the commonly used versions. The major exception is the Twelve Bens ('Pins' on the maps, but I cannot abide the term 'Pins').

GETTING TO ATLANTIC IRELAND

BY PUBLIC TRANSPORT

Working from north to south, there are train stations in Derry, Sligo, Westport, Galway, Tralee and Killarney. These stations are served from points further east, notably Dublin, Rosslare Harbour and Cork. Generally speaking the train service is not frequent.

The bus service is more frequent, with the national carrier Bus Eireann running frequent services to most parts of the country. The express services (timetables 1 to 80) are the ones to choose if you want to travel long distances, though you may also be able to use them to get to the start of routes. In addition to Bus Eireann, private carriers serve some locations and are generally less expensive.

BY CAR
Little need be said about the road system that is not obvious from a glance at a road map. Suffice to say that the road infrastructure is poor by European standards. There are short stretches of motorway which mercifully by-pass some of the main towns. Keep to the main (N) roads if possible as the signposting on other roads is more than poor.

GETTING AROUND ATLANTIC IRELAND
BY BUS
If you are using public transport you will normally travel by Bus Eireann local bus (these will stop anywhere as long as it is safe to do so; they are given in tables 100 upwards in the timetable). Bus Eireann timetable numbers (based on the 1998 timetable) are given with each walk that has a bus within reach of the route itself, perhaps with the help of a lift. The service can be rudimentary so you will have to check the exact schedule beforehand. The peculiar phrase - non-summer - which is used here to describe schedule seasons refers to the period from sometime in September to sometime in May or June (the exact period depends on the route). During the rest of the year the 'summer' timetable applies.

In some parts of the region the services are quite complicated and use place names that do not occur on the maps. In addition, there may be variations within a timetable. I have tried therefore to indicate the road number or the grid reference of some points on the route to help you work out the route for yourself.

BY COACH OR TAXI
If you are a large party it may be more economical to use a coach or taxi rather than public transport. The firms providing such services are listed in the telephone directory.

BY BICYCLE
There are many places where bikes may be hired and you will find the current list in the golden pages of the telephone directory. Don't forget that, if you have only one car, you can use a bike to make A to B walks. As well as arranging that A and B are not too far apart, try to ensure that the bike journey will not be all uphill and that you are not cycling into the prevailing westerly winds.

HITCHHIKING
This is a time-honoured way of getting round all over rural Ireland. However, if you are dripping wet and carrying a bulky rucksack your chances will not be enhanced. Of course, this is just the time you will really want a lift! Women travelling alone after dark should avoid hitching.

ACCOMMODATION

There is a wide variety of guest accommodation in all areas of the country rang-
ing from luxury hotels, through self-catering houses to bed and breakfast and
youth and other hostels and indeed camping. The high season is July and
August, not particularly good months for walking, and only in these months is
there much pressure on accommodation.

We turn now to specific towns and villages which are good centres for walking.
Most of them indeed are good for holidays in general.

There is no centre which is equally convenient to all the mountains of north
Donegal. There are some villages along the N56 eg Creeslough and Dunfanaghy, which are fairly good centres for some of the mountain areas; Dunlewy
is a more central location but is tiny and has few facilities. To the south Donegal
town is much bigger than the places already mentioned and is ideal for the
Bluestacks but too far off for Slieve League. The bustling fishing town of Killybegs is suitable for this latter area or if you are looking for a small, remote village you could hardly find a more suitable location than Glencolumbkille.

For **Sligo and Leitrim** you have the choice of the large town of Sligo to the
west and Dromahaire, a pretty village, or Manorhamilton to the east. In **Mayo**,
Newport is a good centre for the Nephins and even Achill; Westport, an attractive town is larger and has Mweelrea within reach. Further south is tiny Leenaun, an excellent centre for Mweelrea and the mountains of Connemara; in fact it
is almost surrounded by good walking country. A convenient centre for much of
Connemara is Clifden, the largest town for many miles around, though it may
involve much driving to reach some areas. Smaller but better placed for walking
specific areas of Connemara are Recess, Maum Cross or Maum Bridge. For the
Burren, Ballyvaughan is a good centre for the best of the area.

Kerry and West Cork covers, as we have seen, a extensive area much of it located on long peninsulas; we will have to cover these peninsulas in turn. In
Dingle, Tralee is a big town on the landward side but too far off for most tastes.
Some of the small villages on the northern side of the peninsula, such as Castlegregory or Cloghane are ideal for exploring the whole peninsula. Dingle town
lies on the duller southern side but has excellent facilities.

The choice in *Iveragh* is wide though it is too large to allow any one town to be
the ideal centre for the whole peninsula. Killarney or Killorglin are good centres
for the eastern hills, which include the Reeks, and tiny Glencar is close to the
these hills though understandably with few facilities. On the western edge of the
peninsula are a few small towns along the N71, including Waterville, Cahir-
civeen, Glenbeigh and Sneem, a lovely village. The moderately large town of
Kenmare is an exceptionally well-placed centre for southern Iveragh and for
much of Beara to the south.

Lastly *Beara*. As well as Kenmare, tiny Lauragh and the villages around it are
small but well located. Glengarriff is a fairly large centre and from it you can
cover much of Beara and the mountains of west Cork to the east. For west Cork
(solely) Ballingeary is probably the best centre though the road network in the
area does not facilitate easy access, so long drives are inevitable.

MAPS

The Ordnance Survey's up-to-date 1:50 000 Discovery Series covers the country more than adequately. Since most hill walkers will use this series it is worthwhile pointing out a few of their more important characteristics.

- Cliffs are not explicitly depicted, so you must use your judgement by noting the convergence of contour lines. Contour lines have been omitted altogether in the case of some sections of sea-cliff.
- Forests tend not to be as extensive as depicted. Many firebreaks are shown as forest tracks. In general, 'tracks' on the maps that ignore the lie of the land and are depicted in straight lines are in fact firebreaks. Actual tracks tend to keep to gentle slopes and to wind in zig-zag fashion on steep ones.
- The thin black or grey lines shown in some upland areas are field boundaries of some kind, usually walls or earthbanks.
- Few footbridges are shown; long distance paths are badly depicted.
- The thickness of the lines used to indicate streams usually has little bearing on how wide they actually are. In mountain areas, except after heavy rain, it is usually possible to ford streams.

Other maps may be dealt with more briefly. There are **1:25 000** OS maps to the Reeks in Kerry and the area to its east. Except where there are severe and complex cliff areas which the 1:50 000 maps cannot show adequately because of their scale they might not be worth investing in. However if you feel that the modest investment of a few pounds may make the difference between life and death, by all means buy them! The old half-inch to the mile (**1:126 720**) maps are no longer published, but you can still readily pick up copies. They may be useful in getting to the start of walks and in identifying features likely to be off the bounds of the 1:50 000 maps and even more likely to be off the bounds of the black and white extracts given in this book. There is also a **1:250 000** series, which comes in four sheets and which is useful for overall planning.

SAFETY

I was walking recently with a group on Slieve League in Donegal. The day started fine with excellent visibility but as we neared the summit cloud descended and everything - cliff edge, summit cairns, path - disappeared within a few minutes. I got talking to a German foursome who were also climbing the mountain. After some discussion it transpired that they had no compass. They claimed initially to have a map but it soon turned out that not only was it a road map, but that it was back at their car! They hadn't the foggiest (pardon the pun) idea of how to get down. I was of course happy to lead them to safety and they were more than happy to be led.

I mention this anecdote because too many walkers (especially Continentals), think that there is no need for safety precautions in a country where the highest mountain is a puny 1039m. Do not be misled by such seemingly insignificant heights! Irish mountains are wild, remote and worthy of respect. It is noteworthy that a high proportion of the fatal accidents in recent years has been suffered by visitors who did not realise the conditions they were to face.

But let's not be too timid. If you take reasonable precautions and do not try walking in conditions for which you are unprepared, you will enjoy your time in the mountains and return to base safely and with a sense of having achieved something worthwhile.

So, what are reasonable precautions?

- You will get some idea of what to expect on each route from the section on 'Difficulties'. Of course, conditions vary greatly depending on the weather but you can assume that unless the route is entirely or almost entirely on road, track or path you should wear walking boots.
- This section will also give you an idea of how hard it will be to navigate round the route, but remember that the easiest route to follow in bad visibility may be harder than the hardest in good. Cloud and fog make all the difference to navigation. As well as the obvious lack of visibility they are disorienting and distorting, so that what is in reality a minor hill near at hand will appear through cloud like a major mountain much further away.
- Leave word at base of where you intend to go and what time you intend to be back. Get a weather forecast before you go.
- It is definitely prudent not to walk alone and better to have at least four persons. This allows one to stay with the victim if there is an accident and two to try to get help. If the worst comes to the worst, you can summon the mountain rescue by phoning 112 or 999.

WHAT TO CARRY WITH YOU

If you were to carry all the equipment that some experts advise, you would be so weighed down that you wouldn't be able to walk.

The most important item to get right are boots, as mentioned above. Apart from that there are only a few things that you really must carry. These include food and a flask with a hot liquid, a whistle and a map and compass. (As said above, the map extracts given in this guide will generally do instead of the map itself.) Map and compass are no good if you do not know how to use them! Unless the day looks uncommonly settled and likely to remain so, you should take a waterproof. Lastly, you need a rucksack to put everything else in. Anything else is optional or depends mainly on the weather and the route.

RIGHTS OF WAY AND GOOD CONDUCT

Nearly all the land over which you walk, the major exceptions being the way-marked paths and the small areas covered by the national parks, belongs to someone and *you are his or her uninvited guest*. Landowners are generally trusting folk and will not object to your walking across their land. However in recent years there have been a small but increasing number of worrying clashes between walkers and landowners, and keep out signs where such were unthinkable in the past. I have tried to steer you clear of hostile areas but no one knows where problems might next arise. If you come across a hostile sign, particularly at the start of the route, you might try talking to the landowner rather than giving up. Perhaps the sign is not intended for you, particularly if you are taking heed of the following points:

- Respect the privacy of the occupants of houses. If you have to walk through a farmyard, ask permission and do so quietly.
- Do not take dogs into sheep rearing country, that is nearly everywhere in the mountains.
- Do not stand on fence wire as this may irretrievably damage it. If you have to cross stone walls, do not dislodge stones.
- Leave gates just as you found them. Climb them at the hinged end.
- Do not litter the mountains - or anywhere else for that matter. You would be doing a singular service to other hill walkers if you would remove some litter that you find in remote areas such as mountain summits.

THEY'RE YOUR MOUNTAINS TOO - GET INVOLVED!

I wish I could say that the beauty of Ireland's mountains was reflected in the care and attention that we, the Irish people, pay to our environment. Alas, it isn't. There is no need to elaborate, except to state that because in these pages I have usually not mentioned specific instances of littering and dumping, this does not mean that I have not noticed them or have not been saddened by them

I wish there were a simple solution to this, which is caused both by an ingrained couldn't-care-less attitude on the part of too many people and an unwillingness on the part of the responsible authorities to enforce laws. All I can suggest is that you get involved in any organisation that tries to look after the environment and that if you are in a walking club that you ensure that there is an active conservation group and get involved in it.

USEFUL CONTACTS

Irish Bus/Bus Eireann, Busaras, Store Street, Dublin 1. ☎ 01-836 6111.
Irish Rail/Iarnrod Eireann ☎ 01-836 6222.
Independent Holiday Hostels, 57 Lr Gardiner St, Dublin 1. ☎ 01-836 4700.
IYHA/ An Oige, 61 Mountjoy Street, Dublin 7. ☎ 01-830 4555.
Mountaineering Council of Ireland, House of Sport, Longmile Road, Dublin 12.
        ☎ 01-450 9845.
Ordnance Survey of Ireland, Phoenix Park, Dublin 8. ☎ 01-820 6100.

ROUTE 1: ERRIGAL FROM THE NORTH

An unusual approach through varied terrain to Errigal (751m), the most distinctive mountain in Ireland. After climbing the mighty, scree-sloped cone the route traverses two less distinguished peaks before returning along the shores of Altan Lough. A fairly tough but enjoyable route.

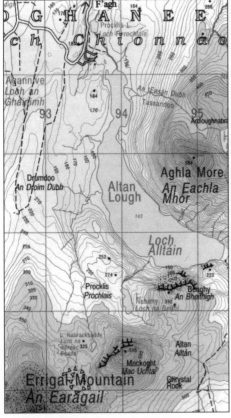

Getting There: From the centre of Falcarragh (GR 9332) take the road south (left if coming from Dunfanaghy), ignore a turn right after 0.4 miles and turn next right after another 0.7 miles. Fork left uphill after another 2.6 miles and park shortly on waste ground just past the fish farm gates (GR 936258). This point may also be reached from Gortahork.

Bus: The Swilly bus (☎ 074-22863) to Gortahork.

Walking Time: 6 hours (distance 15km, climb 850m) allowing a half-hour over Naismith for rocky terrain.

Difficulties: Some boulder-hopping and soggy bogland.

Map: Sheet 1.

Route: Walk onward along the road until it shortly swings right. Cross a stile on the left here and take the track beyond through moorland. This is the dullest part of the route, though the views east to the Aglas and Altan Lough are magnificent. After a long 3km, and here the scree slopes of Errigal dominate the skyline ahead, the track comes to an end, leaving the weary traveller to traverse the bogland without even its modest help.

As you head southward directly for Errigal the slope finally steepens and the ground underfoot is somewhat drier and when you reach the foot of its scree slopes you will have to judge for yourself whether to attempt the direct approach to the summit (see below). If not keep to the left of the high ground to enter a fascinating area of rocky hummocks lying between the base of Errigal and nearby

Mackoght, keeping more of it on your left than right, especially if you wish to climb Errigal. This is not an area where you can make quick progress, unless you want to risk a crocked ankle.

Climb the slabs at the southern end of the hummocky area, veering right at the crest of the ridge to reach the two cairns marking the stony path to the summit - and the only easy way of reaching the summit. This path takes you into a terrain of extensive scree slopes. It's a simple vertigo-free progress; within 5-10 minutes of its end at the summit you attain the crest of a ridge where the path is marked by a set of cairns, into one of which is set the Joey Glover memorial, a noted hill walker murdered by the IRA in one of its many 'mistakes'.

The summit (751m, 3 hours) consists of two tiny peaks about 30m apart, joined by a narrow ridge. With the mountain's surrounds at your feet, this is a superb viewpoint. Slieve Snaght, the huge dome to the south, is the most prominent, but on good days you should easily be able to pick out Benbulben to the south, to the left a plateau, its right side falling precipitously to the plains.

Retrace your steps from the summit to the two cairns noted earlier and then follow the rocky ridge all the way to Mackoght (555m). In poor visibility this is a difficult summit to find, as it has a few rocky high points, each with a cairn. However, what is unmistakable are the steep scree slopes along its northern side. To avoid these, descend initially east for a few hundred metres and then climb north to the bogland forming the hump of Beaghy (395m), watching out, as you reach its gently sloping summit, for scree slopes on *its* northern side. Beaghy's one attraction is the excellent view it offers over Altan Lough, with the Aghlas towering behind.

From Beaghy descend north-east to cross a narrow stream close to a curiously remote tower set in abandoned fields at the eastern end of Altan Lough. Navigational problems, such as they were, are now behind because all you have to do now is walk the north-east shore of the broad lough. There is a path most of the way along the shore traversing the narrow ground below Aghla More. You will have to pick your way through scree slopes reaching to the lakeshore at one point, but otherwise it is an easy 3km walk giving good views of Errigal and its satellites. When you reach the northern end of the lake you should be able to easily wade across as the river is wide and shallow. On the far side pick up a track which ends on tarmac. Turn right here for the nearby start.

Adventurous Variation: If scree slopes hold no terror for you it looks feasible (I haven't tried it!) to climb directly to Errigal's summit from the northern side.

Tourist Variation: You can climb Errigal from the south-east starting on the R251 0.5 miles west of the gate pillar for Altan Farm (easily missed!) and 1.6 miles east of the side turn right (as you drive east) signposted 'Poisoned Glen'. There are several other places along the road west of the Altan Farm pillar where you can park and which are almost equally good starting points.

Climb to the summit initially following posts to find the path up the south-east side. Walk the main route to the tower on Altan Lough; here take a track back to the R251 and turn right for the start. The walking time is 4.5 hours (distance 8km, climb 680m). ∎

ROUTE 2: DOOISH

At 652m, Dooish is the highest point in a line of bare and rocky mountains, none particularly prominent, in the part of the Derryveagh Mountains reaching north-east from Slieve Snaght. The route starts at scenic Lough Beagh, focus of Glenveagh National Park, and traverses much of the best of these mountains.

Getting There: Before you go, read the note below. The entrance to the Park, 7 miles (11km) south of Creeslough at GR 0323, is well signposted.

Walking Time: 6 hours (distance 15km, climb 580m), including about 0.75 hours for boggy terrain.

Difficulties: Lots of wet ground, which may be unexpectedly energy sapping. Navigation is generally easy though there are long stretches without distinct features. Take care around the cliffs and steep ground north-west of Lough Beagh.

Map: Sheet 6.

Route: From the Castle walk between the outbuildings to reach a clear track which runs for about 3km along the south-east shore of Lough Beagh, giving lovely views of the lake and beyond. At its end continue on the track for about 1km it to reach a whitewashed cottage and ford the river on the right here. Walk across boggy ground to reach a path on the near side of the majestic Astelleen Waterfall close by across the narrow valley.

It's a highly scenic - but strenuous - climb by the waterfall and this may compensate for the strain on tired legs. At length, having worked your way round crags near its top, you will find yourself in a high, bare, and mercifully gently sloping valley. Follow the stream north-west for about 1.5km, at which point the main stream veers sharply to the right as it descends. Here climb steeply, at last out of soggy country and into more rocky terrain, directly north to Dooish. Crowned by a well-constructed cairn and with cliffs on its northern face, Dooish (652m, 3.5 hours) commands good views especially towards the Errigal-Muckish range, views which are enhanced if you walk a few metres north to the cliffs.

Drop steeply from here to Lough Aleahan. There is a long narrow cleft starting just south-east of the lough and running north-east parallel to the general trend of the range. (In its floor is a small rocky mound (pt 360m at GR 003222), a useful landmark if you need reassurance farther on.) Keeping to the north-west of this cleft, cross the bare rocky erratic-strewn plateau of Saggartnadooish, and continue over similar terrain to climb pt 391m. From here descend to Misty Lough North and South in turn, both snuggling in wet country south of Kingarrow.

From here to the Visitor Centre the object is to keep as far away from Lough Beagh as possible, as the nearer to the lake you walk the wetter the ground and the higher the tussocks. At length you will reach a gate at the western edge of a mature pine wood. From here, it is a short stroll by track back to the Centre.
Short Variation: From the Castle you can walk for miles and miles through glorious scenery along the initial track but you must return by the same route. Ideal for a bad day!
Note: From September to February inclusive you must get permission from the Park authorities if you intend to leave tracks and paths (☎ 074-37088).

Cars must be left at the Visitor Centre from where, in the summer, you can take a bus to the Castle. In winter you face an additional walk of 3.5km. ■

ROUTE 3: THE AGHLAS

Lying between Errigal and Muckish, the three graceful cones of the Aghlas enfold Lough Feeane. All three offer excellent views of both peaks, as well as further afield. Approached from the north they form a memorable and what is more a natural circuit, the latter a rarity in this area.

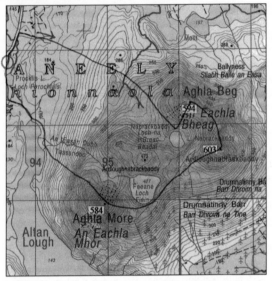

Getting There: From the centre of Falcarragh (GR 9332) take the road south (left if coming from Dunfanaghy), ignore a turn right after 0.4 miles and turn next right after another 0.7 miles. Fork left uphill after another 2.6 miles and park shortly on waste ground just past the fish farm gates (GR 936258). This point may also be reached from Gortahork. **Bus:** The Swilly bus (☎ 074-22863) to Gortahork.

Walking Time: 4 hours (distance 9km, climb 700m).

Difficulties: Boggy terrain in the lower ground but otherwise excellent. Easy navigation.

Map: Sheets 1 and 2.

Route: Walk back along the road from the parking place to cross the first bridge. Take the first turn right to a nearby farmhouse (ask permission to continue) and beyond it walk south-east using what tracks you can find to reach the shores of Nabrackbaddy Lough. This initial stretch to the lough is undoubtedly boring, so you will be pleased to reach the lake and contemplate the trio of fine peaks which rise all around.

The first climb is a direct one north-east through occasional patches of scree to the huge cairn on Aghla Beg (564m, 1.75 hours) from where the view is magnificent, encompassing a wide range of lovely mountains in nearly all directions. The second of the Aghlas lies over high, easily traversed ground to the south-east. This Aghla (603m) is unnamed on the maps, but in spite of this slight the views from this, the highest of the three, are just as good as from Aghla Beg.

The descent is through peat hag country towards the large Lough Feeane. From close to the shores of the lake the ascent to Aghla More (584m, 2.75 hours) is obvious, a stiff one at this late stage in the day.

From the small cairn on Aghla More a little care is needed on the descent to avoid scree on the south-western and northern sides. Walk initially north-west from the cairn, and after a few hundred metres you will have greater choice in picking an easy route to the shores of Altan Lough, where slow progress ensues through difficult haggy ground.

Walk to the northern end of Altan Lough where you can cross by fording the river close to the lake (wet feet may result, though at this late stage it should not be too discomforting). Take the track running north along the opposite shore. This ends at a gate; turn right to reach the nearby parking place. ■

Errigal and the Aghlas (Route 1)

The quartzite dome of Slieve Snaght dominates the Derryveagh Mountains, whose rocky crest is riven by low, transverse, parallel cliffs. These cliffs contribute to making this some of the most difficult - and rewarding - terrain in Donegal. There are several possible routes but this one taking in the Poisoned Glen is probably the best of the lot.

Getting There: Start at the derelict church just south of the R251 in Dunlewy (GR 929190). There is plenty of room to park hereabouts. **Bus:** The Swilly service (☎ 074-22863) to Gweedore and Gortahork.

Walking Time: 4.75 hours (distance 12km, climb 710m).

Difficulties: Easy underfoot until near the end where much boggy terrain has to be endured. In good visibility there should be few navigational difficulties especially with Errigal's huge cone to act as a landmark. In bad weather navigation is difficult as far as the high ground to Lough Slievesnaght, a useful landmark.

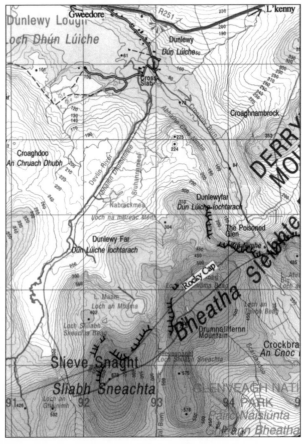

Map: Sheet 1.

Route: From the start you can see most of the route with the great silvery dome of Slieve Snaght prominently rising amidst expanses of bare grey rock. An awe-inspiring sight! Walk down the road from the church to take the track at the nearby hairpin bend. This leads across a bridge and from there you can follow the stream on the right into the Poisoned Glen. As you advance over level, boggy ground the steep grey rocky walls of the Glen close in on both sides and ahead, seemingly leaving the inward route as the only escape.

Not so. Keep by the stream to the end of the valley, where it (the stream) takes a decided right turn in the direction of flow. Cross it here and climb the grassy ramp directly ahead; it is a tough but not vertigo-inducing ascent to the top of the cliffs and to a rocky rib overlooking Lough Atirrive Big (1.5 hours).

The stretch from here to Lough Slievesnaght to the south-west is a difficult one navigationally in bad weather. It consists of an undulating climb over a flattish peak known locally as Rocky Cap (over 580m), followed by a steep descent to the lake, this progress punctuated by a series of low transverse dykes, some of which shelter tiny lakes. After the indeterminate summit of Rocky Cap, your advance south-west is abruptly terminated by the north-south cliffs which mark its western end. Some of the slabs of rock around here form rough rectangles (one is cantilevered over the void); these are as good an indication as any of the imminence of the cliffs.

It is best to approach the northern end of Lough Slievesnaght from the north-east where a grassy ramp aids the descent to this large lake, a good setting for a rest. From here it is a straight climb to Slieve Snaght (3 hours), which is crowned by a sturdy cairn and from which the views can scarcely be equalled in Donegal, with Errigal, the Aghlas and Muckish and a whole panorama of mountain and coastline to be enjoyed.

Descend south-west from Slieve Snaght to avoid cliffs to the west. This will take you to a col from which you can descend north to reach the right bank of the Devlin River. Follow it at a respectable distance because its banks are swampy and also because it runs in a deep-set ravine sheltering a thick mass of trees and shrubs which could not grow on the open moorland. If you simply must cool off there are delightful pools to be found here and there along its route.

As you near the road you will be forced from the Devlin River by a thick wood, so that you will have to ford a stream on the right. To reach the nearby start, you must cross the initial (and only) bridge of the day.

Short Variation: If you do nothing else, walk into the Poisoned Glen to its end. You then might be tempted to go further! ■

ROUTE 5: HORN HEAD

Splendid sea-cliff scenery on a peninsula facing Tory Island, with good views landward towards Muckish and Errigal. This is a long but easy walk that can be easily shortened by taking one of the several minor roads running through the upland centre of the peninsula.

Getting There: From Dunfanaghy take the signposted road for less than a half-mile to Hornhead Bridge (GR 009375). Park just beyond on waste ground on the right. **Bus:** The Swilly service (☎ 074-22863) to Dunfanaghy.

Walking Time: 6 hours (distance 17km, climb about 480m) for the entire walk, including about a half-hour for difficult terrain. It is particularly hard to judge total climb in an area where climb can so easily be traded for distance.

Difficulties: Some high vegetation but not normally wet. No navigational problems.

Map: Sheet 2. Sea-cliffs in the area are not properly indicated.

Route: The first thing you have to decide is whether to walk anti-clockwise or clockwise, bearing in mind that the more dramatic sea-cliff scenery is on the east. If you think the weather is going to deteriorate (it usually seems to!) walk the route anti-clockwise. As said above you can always retreat to an inland road; since these are closer to the east coast this might be another consideration. I describe the route briefly in the anti-clockwise direction below; if you want to do the walk in the opposite direction, take the path on the near side of Horn Head Bridge and continue west on any useful path or track (a compass bearing might be useful).

Take the road onward and where it leaves the shore and heads upward, walk the beach. Keep to it for about 1km, at which point a small stream issues into the estuary. Don't attempt to head inland until you are safely past this stream as there is impassable vegetation near the shore.

After that the route is simple: there are stretches of path that may be some help but the only sure guide is to keep the gradually developing cliffs on the right. Because of this the route is generally upward: past Little Horn Head, around a deep amphitheatre sheltering a luxuriant foliage from the prevailing strong winds, along the shoulder of Croaghnamaddy, until eventually you reach Traghlisk Point and the majestic Horn Head itself, heralded by the Signal Tower ruins. Cross a stile at the Head to get a better view of the scene (3 hours).

The return along the somewhat less dramatic west side is equally easily described. Descend south-west and then climb Crockaclogher. As you descend again to walk towards Pollaguill Bay, look back to admire the superb Templebreaga Arch, a 20m-high sea arch cut out of the base of Crockaclogher. Pollaguill beach is a good place for a swim, after which short grass and generally good underfoot conditions shorten the stretch to McSwyne's Gun, once a spectacular blowhole, but since its aperture has widened, now much less impressive.

From the north end of Tramore Strand (it's nearly 2km long so you can't mistake it) a spot of compass work may be needed, aiming across the sand dunes to reach the northern side of Hornhead Bridge. Keeping forest on the left you may be lucky enough to pick up a track or path ending at a gate beside the bridge. Once on the road turn left for the car.

Short Variation: The next peninsula to the east, Melmore Head, offers the coastal cliffs and ambience of Horn Head, though on a smaller scale. Take the R248 from Carrigart (GR 1336), turn right at the signpost for the youth hostel, pass the viewing area on the right, turn immediately right, and park in Tranarossan carpark (GR 119419). Gallaghers' (☎ 074-37037) run an evening bus service in the area.

You can walk all the way round the peninsula in about 3 hours (distance 10km, climb about 220m). There is no need for a detailed description of the route. By the way you might like to swim in some of the small beaches around the peninsula, but do not attempt to do so at Boyeegter Bay on the west as there is a strong undertow. ■

An area without 'proper' peaks but instead a rocky, hummocky, treeless terrain with numerous extensive granite slabs, tiny lakes and erratic boulders. This route is the classic approach to the quintessential Blue Stacks. It takes in Lough Belshade, a useful lifeline in bad visibility.

Getting There: From Donegal town, about 7 miles (11km) away, take the road along the west side of Lough Eske, following signs to Harvey's Point Country Hotel. When you reach the sign indicating that it is 1km away, keep straight ahead for 2.5 miles to turn left off the main road at an Ulster Way waymark. You can park here (GR 969861) or drive a further half-mile to a small parking place at the end of tarmac (GR 973870). **Buses:** 30, 64, 69 (express), 480, 494 all to Donegal town. **Walking Time:** 4.5 hours (distance 10km, climb 580m), including nearly an hour for difficult terrain and route finding. This time assumes that you start at the end of tarmac.

Difficulties: A difficult area for navigation, so keep to the safe shores of Lough Belshade if unsure. There are short, easily bypassed sections of cliff towards the end of the unabridged walk. Except after a prolonged drought, the underfoot conditions in the lower parts of the route are exceptionally wet.

Map: Sheet 11.

Route: Take the track northwards, pass forestry on the right and a short distance after, climb a grassy ramp close to the hidden cascade of Doonan Waterfall East, thus eliminating a vee in the track. You now find yourself in a soggy river valley flanked by rocky hillsides, the Corabber River on the right and the Ulster Way track underfoot, the latter about to expire at a small hydro-works.

About 15 minutes from these works you have to find a path heading off left to Lough Belshade. It's not difficult. First watch out for a waymark on a grassy hummock, then a stream flanked by a path which enters the Corabber River at right angles. Follow this path, of which it might be charitably said that it is no wetter than its surrounds, all the way north-west to the lake (1.25 hours).

The lake is a gem, its shores sheltering tiny beaches of yellow sand in secluded coves, its sides guarded in parts by ramparts of granite cliff, behind which the high peaks of the Blue Stacks lie in an arc in all directions except the south-east. It is good place to linger and maybe contemplate the next move.

At least in good weather you can wander where you like, so the following is just one suggestion among many. Use the rough dam to cross the outlet stream from the lake and walk along the north-east shore to a tiny beach at the northern end. From here you can climb steeply, a ravine close on the left and vertical slabs further away, directly into high rock country and so reach pt 642m. Continue along the high ground south-west to pt 626m (2.75 hours). About 250m to its west is a large unmistakable white quartzite outcrop, the one and only beacon in the desert and therefore a good place from which to start the next leg of the route should you be worried about navigation.

From pt 626m (or the outcrop) head almost south, aiming for the headwaters of a stream which empties into Lough Gulladuff. This is the most difficult part of the route, because there are two stretches of cliff overlooking Lough Gulladuff and its sister lakes from their west and north. Neither stretch is more than a few hundred metres long and so they are easy to avoid, but it is better to come down, steeply but on grass, by the stream between them.

At Lough Gulladuff follow the outlet stream through the soggy swamp interspersed with grassy hummocks in which it lies. This will take you over a rocky rampart through which the stream plunges in an impressive cascade. Beyond this cascade descend alongside it to turn right onto the initial track.

Short Variation: Just to remind you that a walk to Lough Belshade is easy navigationally but wet underfoot, and gives you much of the flavour of the Blue Stacks. The walking time is 1.25 hours to the lake and about an hour back. ∎

ROUTE 7: SLIEVE LEAGUE

The sea-cliffs of Slieve League are renowned, partly (I am guessing) because it is possible, without walking more than a few feet from your car, to view the entire stretch of mighty precipice. View but not experience, so get out of your car and make the easy walk to the highest point of these cliffs, the summit of Slieve League (595m). You can of course return by the same route but this one makes an attractive inland alternative.

Getting There: The start is about 14 miles (23km) west of Killybegs. From the town take the R263 to Carrick, turn left in the village, and right at the sign 'Bunglas/The Cliffs' near the post office in Teelin. Continue to the end of the road at GR 558757, passing through a gate on the way. Take it easy: the final stretch of road delights in steep gradients and abrupt twists. **Bus:** 490 to Carrick.

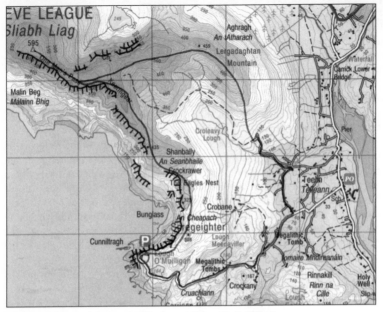

Walking Time: 4.75 hours (distance 13km, climb 770m).

Difficulties: None, except for the mildest of vertigo on the so-called 'One Man's Pass'. Navigation easy and underfoot conditions generally good.

Map: Sheet 10.

Route: If you have a cliff on one side and a path under your feet, as you have on Slieve League, there is little point in describing the route in pernickety detail. Simply take the path upward from the parking place and follow it. At one place (pt 455m) you can, if you wish, keep to the rocky crest of the ridge, but if you don't fancy that keep to the perfectly safe but muddy path winding round to its right.

At length you will reach the eastern summit of Slieve League (over 570m) marked by numerous cairns on a plateau of soft ground, with similar ground (it's your return route, if you choose it) reaching away north-eastward. But for now the route is westward over the aforementioned 'One Man's Pass', which is simply a narrow level path with steep grassy slopes on both sides. Past this is the goal of the route, the trig pillar on Slieve League (595m, 2.25 hours). This is a marvellous viewing point with Benbulben to the south-east, the tiny but high Stacks of Broadhaven off the Mayo coast to the south-west and perhaps the cone of Errigal to be seen off to the north. It's worth walking a little further on to see the Chimneys, a group of high stacks on steep ground seaward.

And so to the return, which is different in character but nothing like as memorable as the outward route. Retrace steps over the 'One Man's Pass' and walk north-east, the corrie of Lough Agh on the left, passing the holy wells and oratory. Drop to a narrow pass to their east and then climb the broad shoulder of

24 Donegal

The Bluestacks (Route 6)

Lergadaghtan Mountain (459m). From here continue south-east to meet, at a set of enclosures, the inland track up Slieve League, sometimes disparagingly called the 'Old Man's Path' (3.75 hours).

From here it is road, but a varied one, all the way to the start. Walk down from the enclosures, turn right at the tee, immediately cross a bridge and where instinct tells you almost infallibly to turn left downhill, turn right uphill. This track leads to the road along which you drove. Turn right onto it for the carpark over 2km away.

Short Variation: If you want sea-cliffs and are in Glencolumbkille (GR 5384), don't on any account miss the cliffs directly to its north. By car, pass the church in the main street on the right, take the next right, turn left at the tee and left again at the next junction. Park at the foot of high ground about a half-mile farther on. Alternatively you can easily walk from the village. Follow the cliff as far as you like but at least as far as Sturrall Head, a magnificent rocky peninsula 3km from the village. Return by the same route or pick up an inland track from around the Signal Tower. ■

ROUTE 8: THE GLENCAR ESCARPMENT

A spectacular ascent to the Benbulben plateau through one of the fearsome gullies in the riven cliffs guarding it. The walk along the edge of the escarpment is easy and entertaining and allows excellent views down into Glencar Lough and across to Castlegal.

Getting There: From *Sligo* take the N15, after over 3 miles (5km) turn right just after Rathcormack church, turn right at the tee over a mile further on and drive another 1.4 miles to park immediately before a prominent guest house on the left (GR 715424). From *Manorhamilton*, you can start at the amenity area at Glencar Lough if you wish (GR 760434). Otherwise, drive the length of Glencar Lough on the left, turn first right and continue for 1.2 miles to park at the guest house. Parking is limited here so do so considerately. The starting point is not conspicuous so pay attention to navigation. **Buses:** 65, 66, 67 (all express), 470 (via Glencar Cross on the N16).

Walking Time: 4.25 hours (distance 13km, climb about 500m) including 5km walk along the road at the end if you haven't a second car.

Difficulties: The ascent into the gully near the start should give little cause for concern unless you suffer from really severe vertigo. Only rough bearings are needed on the plateau that forms much of the route and the track that takes you off it is hard to evade.

Map: Sheet 16.

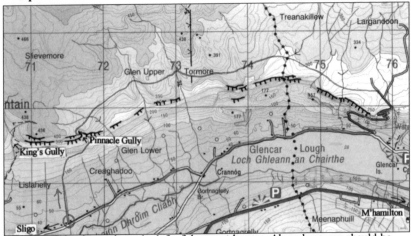

Route: Take the track on the left of the guest house. Along here you should be able to clearly see Pinnacle Gully, the huge semi-detached vertical slab of rock that, a few hundred metres off to the right, forms the upward route.

Where the track ends at a deserted house continue upwards through rushy fields towards steeper ground below the cliffs. Once into unenclosed land turn right

26

and follow a stone wall bordering enclosed land as far as a tiny stream and stone chute issuing from Pinnacle Gully. Don't try to climb until you are abreast of the gully; the steeply sloping ground makes for uncomfortable walking.

Around the bottom of the chute look out for a grassy path that seems to offer an easy way to the gully. So it does, for a while. But its aim is to outflank the cliffs so at some point you must leave it and head directly into the mouth of the gully, the steepest ascent of the day by far. At the gully's mouth cross a fence to enter it, walk steeply upward for a few metres on loose rocks, and then turn left into a passage between the Pinnacle that gives the gully its name (left) and the main face of the cliffs (right). Walk steeply upward to the end of this enclosed passage and then clamber up the gigantic rock steps on the left to emerge, like a rabbit from a burrow, on grass high above the valley floor. Quite an exciting few minutes, I'm sure you'll agree.

There is a short but steep climb from here directly to the undulating ground of the plateau from where lies the prospect of an easy walk with good underfoot conditions and easy navigation all the way east. You can wander along the edge of steep ground and cliffs on the right or you can take a more northerly route thus avoiding some gentle up-and-down climbing; I suggest the former, since the views are going to be better.

As you advance you will meet a few interesting points along the way to chart your progress. After crossing a stream with two ruins on its eastern side, you will cross another spanned by the remains of a dam, and a short time later you will pass under a defunct power line and bucket cable system formerly used for the mines farther north. Along here you should also be able to see great elongated grassy mounds below in the valley on the near side of Glencar Lough, remnants that have slumped from the plateau edge. Nearer at hand you can investigate deep channels in the limestone (don't fall in!). Finally, at the point where you cross into county Leitrim (marked by a dotted line on the map), you will ford a few converging streams surging over horizontal slabs of limestone, where you should easily be able to find fossils. Don't say plateaus are without interest!

After this your still eastward route is over dullish bogland, where you will reach a clear track. Turn right onto it to reach the road running along the shore of Glencar Lough. From here, assuming you haven't a second car you have 5km on tarmac amid attractive scenery. Turn right onto the road and right again at the end of the lake to reach the start. ∎

ROUTE 9: CASTLEGAL
The general rule about the Sligo-Leitrim region that the steep edges are of more interest than the moorland they surround is splendidly contradicted in the Castlegal range just to the east of Sligo town. Hills of no great height (they reach only 463m) they nonetheless form a complex array of flat-topped peaks ringed by low cliffs and steep ground. This walk takes in the western part of the range and gives excellent views over Lough Gill and the Benbulben plateau.

Getting There: From *Sligo* take the N16 for about 3 miles (5km) to pass a black-on-yellow diamond-shaped road sign indicating that the main road turns right with a side road continuing straight ahead. Keep on the N16 here to park carefully at another side road on the left 1.2 miles farther on (GR 719411). From *Manorhamilton* on the N16 look out for the brown sign 'Glencar Lake 2k' and park at the side road on the right 0.4 miles farther on. If you have a second car you might leave it at a junction off the N16 to avoid an unpleasant walk along this usually busy road at the end. This junction (at GR 721396), on the right from Sligo, is 2.4 miles (3.9km) from the junction of the R286 and N16. **Bus:** 470 (via Glencar Cross on the N16).

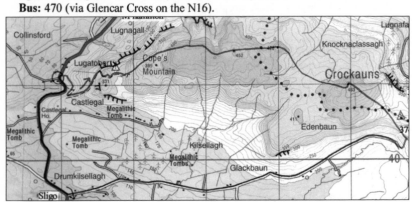

Walking Time: 4.25 hours (distance 12km, climb 600m) for the full walk using only one car. If you have a second and leave it at the junction mentioned above; the distance is reduced to 10km.

Difficulties: With a bewildering array of small peaks the high ground can be rather intimidating in bad visibility. In these conditions the best plan is to head relentlessly east, diverting round obstacles until you descend into lower, wetter ground where there is a prominent isolated house (at about GR 768399).

Map: Sheet 16. The initial track on the route is incorrectly depicted at its lower (western) end.

Route: Cross the road and the gate supported on concrete pillars opposite it, and walk uphill to the far end of the *first* field beyond it to reach a wide but secluded grassy track, difficult to discern at this point. Turn right onto it, thus advancing gently but steadily upward through scattered trees. Keep on it into open ground as it rises right across the western end of Cope's Mountain and finally deposits you at the edge of the plateau close to the cairn on the west top (331m).

Walking east from the west top cross a narrow grassy plain to enter an area of limestone knolls bounded on the north by cliffs and rotting rocky pinnacles overlooking Glencar. The exact route here is immaterial as long as you continue roughly east, but a route close to Glencar (that is more northerly) offers an intermittent path and dramatic cliffscapes.

Beyond this area contour partly round a broad grassy gully which falls towards the western end of Glencar Lough. From about this gully you can explore higher ground to the south taking in pts 452m and 428m, before dropping into wetter lower ground facing Crockauns (463m). Follow the wall running up the right flank of that mountain and where it levels off and peters out in hummocky ground strike off left directly towards the top. A word of warning: the initial wall is clear enough in good weather but there are several walls in the area so in bad visibility do not follow a wall without checking your direction.

Crockauns has a well-built cairn and commands lovely views, that towards the Benbulben Plateau to the north being particularly noteworthy. As you gradually descend east from Crockauns, keep to the high ground and watch out for two grassy hills (374m and over 380m). Aim for the right of the more southerly, perhaps encountering a wall junction as you do so. From about this junction make a steep descent south close to hawthorn bushes to reach the very narrow road of Glackbaun, just wide enough for one car. Turn right and follow it all the way back to the main road, a scenic stretch mostly at the foot of steep ground below Castlegal. If you have not left your car at the junction of the N16 you will have to walk the extra 2km to the start. ■

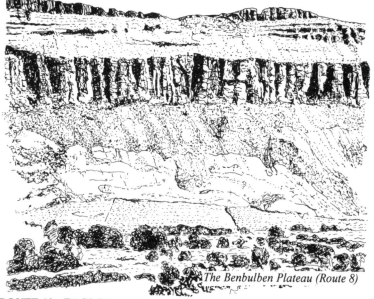

The Benbulben Plateau (Route 8)

ROUTE 10: EAGLES ROCK

A shorter route than route 8, but with somewhat the same character. Its main feature is the strange rock formation called Eagles Rock, a forbidding column of limestone, with several subsidiary columns, rising close to the plateau from which it has become detached.

Getting There: Drive the R280 south from Largydonnell (GR 7951). Pass the church on the left, take the next right, drive to a tee, turn left and park shortly at the ruin on the right (GR 786487). **Bus:** 483 to Park Cross (GR 7952).

Walking Time: 3.5 hours (distance 11km, climb about 380m).

Difficulties: Much boulder hopping at Eagles Rock but otherwise easy. Navigation is simple.

Map: Sheet 16. It places Eagles Rock 1km north-west of its actual location.

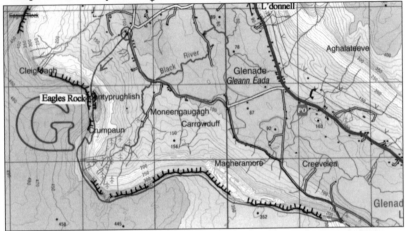

Route: Cross the gate to the right of the ruin and the fence just beyond it. Follow the fence south-west until you are close to the yawning gap between plateau and Rock (its majesty is far from obvious at the start). Walk over boulders to reach the high point between the Rock and the plateau, an awe-inspiring section of the walk and incidentally a good place to look out for fossils.

Descend the increasingly grassy slope from the highest ground between Rock and plateau, walking close to crumbling subsidiary columns and then a hummocky grassy ridge on the left. At or just beyond a stone ruin, the only one hereabouts, you will find a path making a zig-zag approach to the plateau to the west. From here navigation is simple: follow the plateau edge south and then east. Along here you can admire Glenade and later its Lough down on the left as well as some bizarre rock sculptures, miniature Eagles Rocks nearer at hand below the edge of the plateau.

When you come abreast of the western end of Glenade Lough, you will see forest ahead. There is a rough track running alongside it so at any convenient point walk downhill through rough vegetation to turn left onto it. Take it on a straight course downhill to a rough road and turn left onto it. Ignoring obvious cul-de-sacs, take two first turns left to reach the start. ■

ROUTE 11: THE DOONS AND LEEAN

Rising almost from the shores of Lough Gill and close to the town of Sligo are the Doons, a strange area of tiny, steep-sided, flat-topped limestone hills. The route traverses the Doons and climbs part of the bewilderingly varied Castlegal Range behind it. This is an easy circuit that lends itself to several variations. It is also one of the few routes in the area that facilitates a convincing loop.

Getting There: Let's suppose you are at Parkes Castle (GR 7835) on the R286. With it on the right turn next left, drive steeply uphill to a tee, turn left, pass a small church shortly on the left, and take the nearby next right turn. Drive uphill for less than a mile to park at the sandpit (GR 785374), where there is room for several cars. **Buses:** 462, 469 (both run along the R286), 470 (via Leckaun) runs on a road parallel to the R286 and just north of it.

Walking Time: 3.25 hours (distance 8km, climb 560m) but remember that this is an area which lends itself to pottering and variations.

Difficulties: Lots of muddy ground and a few sections of easily avoidable short stretches of cliff. Navigation is easy.

Map: Sheets 16 or 25.

Route: Take the track to the left of the sandpit and walk past the forested base of one of the Doon hills to shortly fork left and pass through a farmyard. Continue upwards on the track beyond the yard into pleasant open country with the plateau of Keelogyboy on the left and the sharp prow of Sramore (about 410m), the first peak to be climbed, on the right.

The track ascends into high ground at the base of Keelogyboy, much further north than depicted on the map. Unfortunately this does not facilitate the Sramore-bound, so to avoid an unnecessary descent into comparatively low ground on the right we must leave the track before it rises too high on Keelogyboy in order to climb east to Sramore. However do not attempt a direct attempt on Sramore as there are short but unclimbable stretches of cliff close to its south-facing prow. Instead climb diagonally left through high heather. Incidentally, as you reach the rocky band near the top of this climb, you should be able to find fossilised rocks.

Once on the heathery plateau that is Sramore it's well worthwhile making a there-and-back to the prow to the south for the excellent views of Lough Gill and the hills beyond it. After that, retrace your steps to the northern end of the plateau and then descend towards the grassy hummocks to the east. Note the change in vegetation as you reach the northern end of Sramore: as you cross the fence on the descent the high heather is abruptly replaced by grass. There are no sheep to the south of the fence!

Climb the grassy hummocks and then walk south-east to the corner of forest, a sad spindly group of trees, but since it is the only forest for miles around, a good reassurance feature. Keep the forest on the left as its edge runs east but where it swings north cross several fences (carefully) to descend east to a broad valley separating grassy Leean (417m) from the rest of the range.

The valley is wet and eroded so you will probably be glad to reach a barely noticeable mound to the west of Leean, from where Glencar Lough comes into view to the north-west. Then climb to the trig pillar marking the summit from where Benbo and the town of Manorhamilton are clearly visible.

Descend south from the summit to cross a tiny area of limestone pavements and beyond it reach a track. That's the end of rough ground for the day as from here on the route is on road or track through a wide variety of country: small upland fields, grassy hummocks, lines of trees and hedges and finally some of the small hills of the Doons. I hope this compensates for the occasional muddy stretch.

Back to the route. Turn left downhill onto the track to cross a river, go up hill and down dale beyond it to turn acutely right onto another track. Walk downhill for a short distance to meet a road at a U-turn and continue straight ahead. In the next 10 or more minutes you will pass two long driveways on the right, and after them you should turn right onto a usually muddy track which curves left

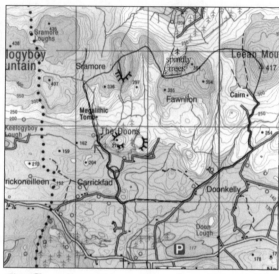

round a hill before reaching the road up which you drove. Turn right onto it for the nearby start.

Variations: You could climb the plateau of Keelogyboy or even Hangman's Hill from the initial track of the route. You can shorten the route by returning from the corner of forest mentioned above or by not climbing Leean. ■

ROUTE 12: BUNNACUNNEEN

The Bunnacunneen range is actually just into Galway but is included here for convenience (and because it seems like part of Mayo!). A horseshoe-shaped range with soggy higher ground, its main interest lies in the enclosed, grassy, steep-sloped valleys which lie at its foot. This short route explores one of these valleys before tackling its highest peak, Bunnacunneen itself (575m).

Getting There: Turn off the R336 at Griggins (GR 9256), that is turn right if coming from Maum Bridge - it's the only turn for miles. Drive for a few hundred metres to a dilapidated hut on the left where there is room for a few cars.

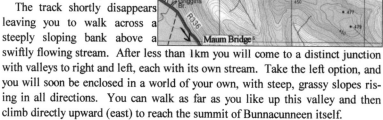

Buses: 419 (non-summer only, via Maum Bridge to Griggins (GR 9256).), 420 (the summer equivalent of 419).

Walking Time: 3.5 hours (distance 10km, climb 620m), including 5km on road.

Difficulties: None.

Map: Sheet 38.

Route: Walk up the road, shortly taking the first track on the right serving a farmhouse. Pass by its side (quietly) and take the now steeply rising track into the narrow valley behind it.

The track shortly disappears leaving you to walk across a steeply sloping bank above a swiftly flowing stream. After less than 1km you will come to a distinct junction with valleys to right and left, each with its own stream. Take the left option, and you will soon be enclosed in a world of your own, with steep, grassy slopes rising in all directions. You can walk as far as you like up this valley and then climb directly upward (east) to reach the summit of Bunnacunneen itself.

Bunnacunneen (575m) is a good viewpoint: the Maumturks and the farther off Twelve Bens to the west, the Devilsmother and Mweelrea to the north-west, the Maumtrasna plateau to the north and the rest of the Bunnacunneens of which this peak forms the modest apex, reaching in two long spurs eastward.

From the summit head north along the narrow spur to Currarevagh (416m). Along here, beyond the cliffs close on your right, you can admire the mighty northern flanks of the Bunnacunneens, which fall hundreds of metres in grassy slopes, broken by the occasional crag, towards the shores of Lough Nafooey. An impressive sight. By the way, don't worry about finding Currarevagh itself as it hardly rises above the general level among the occasional crags along this spur.

Keep on the spur as you descend, bogland on both sides and the large Lough Nafooey off to the right, till you reach a road close to a tiny hamlet. Turn left onto it to reach the 'main' road. The rest of the walk, all 4km of it, is on a remote road through windswept bogland but not without interest. Turn left onto this road (or you may consider it straight ahead *uphill*) walk it to the crest of the hill, passing an impressive waterfall on the way set amidst dense vegetation. Beyond the crest the road appears to have reached a dead end amid bogland, but do not fear, it eventually swings left towards Griggins and the start. ■

ROUTE 13: MWEELREA

The pyramid of Mweelrea (814m) and its satellites rise from a high, undulating, contorted, broad ridge bounded in places by fearsome corries. It dominates the northern side of the sinuous fiord of Killary Harbour and the western side of the narrow R335 road from where its giant north-eastern corrie is seen to perfection. The route reaches the summit from this corrie: a memorable approach to a lovely walking area.

Getting There: Start on the R335 at the northern end of the large Doo Lough (GR 828695), where there are several places to park along the road. This point is about 21 miles (34km) south of Westport (via Louisburgh) and 11 miles (17km) north of Leenaun. If you have a second car leave it 2.5 miles (4km) south (GR 845666) at a rough quarry on the west of the road.

Walking Time: 7.25 hours (distance 17km, climb 1180m), including a 4km road walk. One slow, steep descent is partly compensated for by this road walk.

Difficulties: A long strenuous walk though navigationally straightforward in good weather. In bad visibility the problems are obvious from the map: you have to get off the steep ground roughly eastwards, but this way is partly barred by a line of cliffs. So, take especial care on the descent.

Map: Sheet 37.

Route: From the road walk along the sandy northern shore of Doo Lough, and ford the river flowing between it and Glencullin Lough or cross it on a wide bridge about 100m from Doo Lough. Then continue initially south-westwards following a stream and then veer southwards following its tributary, the general idea being to reach a grassy ramp running upwards from left to right across the north-east facing section of the corrie wall ahead.

The walk up the ramp is steep, but this is a small matter, since with frowning cliffs on the right overlooking the corrie bottom and the great soaring, jagged corrie wall on the left, this is a memorable ascent. Nor is it vertigo-inducing, as there is only one short section at the top where a moderately steep slope must be crossed, and here there is a narrow path.

The ramp deposits the walker at a cairn (2.25 hours) at the lowest point of the corrie wall (it's worth noting the cairn as you will need it for the return). From here it is only 400m to the two adjacent summits on Ben Bury (795m). Then walk generally west keeping cliffs close on the right to reach a shallow col facing Mweelrea, a walk offering marvellous views in all directions. From this col there is a stiff climb to the summit itself. On the way it is worth diverting left to view the steep corrie holding Lough Bellawaum. Strangely Mweelrea's summit is unimpressive, a grassy mound without even a trig pillar, but the views are magnificent, covering a whole circuit of sea, island, fiord and mountain (3.5 hours).

Return directly to the cairn at the top of the ramp (in bad visibility retrace exactly the Mweelrea-bound steps). From it walk east generally uphill, immense corrie cliffs on the left, to climb eventually a short but stiff 60m to the great tooth-shaped peak of Ben Lugmore (803m). Still following the cliff edge just beyond Lugmore's summit swing abruptly left (north-east) onto a grassy plateau.

From here all the way to the road at a point just south of Doo Lough head roughly east, at first keeping close to cliffs and later steep ground on the left. On this course you will make one short climb before a particularly demanding descent at the end of a long day. It is through thick vegetation, partly broken up by long sandstone slabs. As you near the road head towards a new stone house at about GR 845666 (it's on the far bank of the stream). Close to it turn left to follow a fence to a gate just above a causeway at Doo Lough. Cross the stream here and walk to the road. If no car is waiting, there is nothing for it but to turn left and walk 4km to the start. ∎

Sea-cliffs - high, rugged, fearsome- form the focus of interest of this walk. It takes in the narrow headland of Achill Head; bulky Croaghaun (688m), sliced from summit to sea to give the highest sea-cliffs in Ireland; and finally the steep-sided corries of two mountain lakes.

Getting There: The start is at the far west of Achill Island, at Keem Bay (GR 562045). This is 34 miles (54km) west of Newport, and so not the easiest place in the world to reach. From Achill Sound keep to the main road for 14 miles (23km) and park at the large carpark above the beach, not the one close to it.

Buses: 66 (express), 440, 441 to Dooagh.

Walking Time: 5 hours (distance 13km, climb 980m).

Difficulties: Generally good underfoot conditions. The only minor spot of navigational uncertainty is pointed out below. In high wind take care near cliffs!

Map: Sheet 30. The initial track shown on the map does not exist.

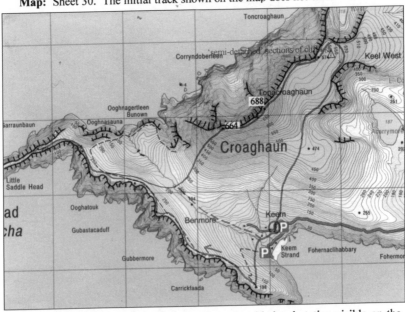

Route: From the carpark climb directly to the old signal station visible on the hill to the south. From here simply keep the sea-cliffs on the left over two mighty mounds (or rather half-mounds, since the seaward side falls almost vertically to the sea). The cliffs, impressive from the start, get even more impressive as you walk towards Achill Head, a bony finger pointing into the ocean. Look east along here to the mighty cliffs of Croaghaun, best viewed from this side.

Only the fear of a terrible death caused by plunging into the foaming sea below need deter you from scrambling along the developing knife-edge towards the end of the Head. At some point however discretion will overcome valour and you will have to turn back. When you do so, gradually descend left from the cliff-edge to reach two muddy lakes (at GR 547050) perched between valleys to north-west and south-east. For the short variation, walk down the bottom of the valley to the south-east to reach the start (total walking time 3 hours).

Achill Head (Route 14)

If however you want to do the whole route you will be pleased to hear that you are ideally located to start the assault on Croaghaun to the north-east but maybe less pleased to observe that the route looks decidedly steep. Steep it certainly is, through increasingly rock-strewn terrain, but is hardly going to cause vertigo. If nonetheless you are scared veer right where the slope is a little easier.

The assemblage of boulders marking the south-west summit of Croaghaun (664m) gives a lovely viewpoint; even lovelier views of the sections of huge sea-cliffs stretching away to the north-east await. So, keeping the cliffs on the left walk to the north-east top (688m) and onward, still following the cliff edge.

After you pass two 'semi-detached' sections of cliff that have resulted in impressive gullies between them and the main cliff look out for the rim of the corrie containing Bunnafreva Lough West. In bad weather make sure you reach it, because from there you must reach the great double corrie containing Lough Acorrymore only a few hundred metres away to the south. Keep the steep slopes of this corrie on the left as you advance across fairly boggy terrain (a rough compass bearing on the carpark may be prudent). This bearing will take you over comparatively featureless, though safe terrain right back to the start.

Short Variation: The route has been described above. It offers marvellous sea-cliff views with comparatively little climbing. You might also consider following the tops of the north-facing sea-cliffs as far as you like, then walk to the two muddy lakes, and thence to the start. ■

ROUTE 15: GLENDAHURK (NEPHINS)

If you intend to walk only one route in the Nephins, this is the one. A neat circuit high above the forested and wet valley of Glendahurk, it offers excellent, varied views with fairly good underfoot conditions for much of its length and with an exhilarating stretch about 1km long as a climax.

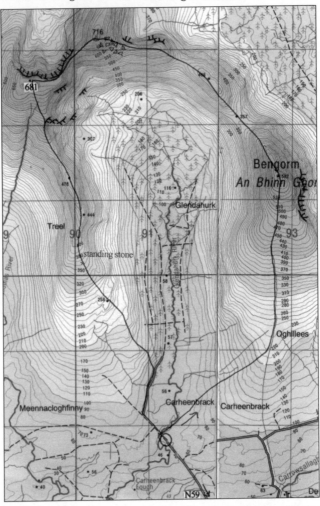

Getting There: From *Newport* take the N59 towards Mulrany. Keep on it for 3.9 miles (6.3km), measured from the sign for the youth hostel. Turn right onto a side road here (it's very obscurely signposted 'Carheenbrack'). If you miss this turn you will know because you will pass a statue on the left. In this case turn back; don't continue on to take the next side road right as it is extremely narrow.

From *Mulrany*, watch out for the statue on the right, take the next turn left. In both cases drive along the side road for a mile to park at a deserted building just before a bridge (you can't drive much further) (GR 913978). **Buses:** 66 (summer only express stopping at Mulrany and Newport), 440, 441 (both non-summer only).

Walking Time: 5.75 hours (distance 14km, climb 1020m).

Difficulties: There is a short stretch of very easy scrambling with a little exposure. Navigational difficulties are minor.

Map: Sheets 30 and 31. The maps exaggerate the extent of forestry tracks; the only actual track (as opposed to firebreaks) runs north-south on the west of the Glendahurk River.

Route: Walk towards the bridge, cross the gate on the right just before it and follow the river upsteam for a few hundred metres. After this, there is nothing for it but to walk north-east over bogland and so reach the southern spur of Ben Gorm. Apart from the views (best to the rear over Clew Bay), the odd feature of this ascent is provided by the improbable stream which runs plumb down the crest of the spur, and which appears on the map to defy the law of gravity.

Keep with this stream to its source and then head directly north to the summit of Ben Gorm (582m), passing on the way slabby cliffs on the right, an indication of sterner country ahead. Beyond Ben Gorm head roughly north-west, keeping to the crest of the undulating ridge, though one with considerably more ups than downs. There is nothing undulating about the climb after it to the trig pillar on the summit of Corrannabinnia (716m, 3.75 hours). With stretches of cliff on the right, it is steep and lengthy and is through a considerable boulder field.

Corrannabinnia stands at the centre of the Nephin Begs, with fine spurs and ridges in three directions. You have just laboured up the south-east spur. To the north is Glennamong, to which a there-and-back extension might be worthwhile if you have the time. But it is the ridge to the South West Top (681m), the one we must now traverse, which should claim our attention.

There is a steep descent over rocks to a grassy col, followed by a clamber around and over rocks, the ascent forming the tough part of the route. With the choice of sheer cliffs on the right and merely steep ground on the left, it doesn't require much intelligence to keep left if vertigo threatens. A dramatic and memorable section.

The rest is easy. The South West Top is simply a level grassy area; in bad weather do not waste time trying to find a summit. From there head south, keeping a wary eye for cliffs on the left. Along here the ground underfoot is soggy, but the views towards Clew Bay with Croagh Patrick beyond are magnificent. There is one navigational aid: a standing stone (or more probably a stone that happens to be standing) whose approximate position is shown on the map.

After 3km or so along this spur, forestry nears on the left along with a track that accesses this forest. Turn right onto it, walk to a tee, turn left and walk to the nearby start. ■

Across the R335 from Mweelrea the high western side of the small Ben Gorm massif falls in long grassy slopes to the road. From this side runs a series of east-reaching spurs, some long, some short, with impressive corries tucked into their western end. This walk takes in two of the longer spurs and Ben Gorm itself, at 700m the highest point in the range. A lovely walk that can easily be varied. Try however to avoid the lower, squelchy ground.

Getting There: From *Westport* take the N59 for over 5 miles (8km), turning right here at the sign 'Drimmin 8km'. Drive for another 9.5 miles (15km) to park at a forestry entrance on the right (GR 896674). From *Leenaun* (but see also the variation) take the N59 north, turn left onto the R335, turn right after about 8 miles (14km), the only turn for miles, and park at the forest entrance after over 3 miles (5km). Both journeys are through lovely scenery. **Bus:** 61 (express to Cushlough on the N59).

Walking Time: 4.5 hours (distance 11km, climb 840m), though there are several easily devised shorter (or indeed longer) variations.

Difficulties: Some navigational uncertainty close to Ben Gorm itself, otherwise only wet ground in the valleys to worry about.

Maps: Sheet 37.

Route: Walk east along the road for a few metres and use conveniently placed stones to cross a fence on the right. Turn right (west) immediately to cross a bridge over a minor stream and then walk onwards to reach a much wider one. Follow this stream south-west by high banks to reach Glendavuck, a remote valley which reaches over 2km west into the Ben Gorms.

After you pass between these banks you will see a low point in the spur ahead (south) and as you will already have guessed this is the first objective. Cross the stream, one definitely of the 'wade across' (it's wide and shallow), rather than the 'jump across' (narrow but deep) variety. Climb moderately steeply to the col, and now with the Devilsmother close to the south-east, the Maumturks to the south and the haystacks of the Twelve Bens to their right, you can start the exhilarating march west to Ben Gorm.

Along the length of the spur progress is easy, with rough ground and increasingly slabs underfoot. Simply follow the crest predominantly west in a gentle curve to the left. As you near its end you should be able to see two fine rockbound corries to right and left, the latter holding Lugaharry Lough.

A large cairn, about 2m high, close to the edge of cliffs to the north marks the summit plateau of Ben Gorm but not the summit itself, which is about 200m away to the west. At the summit (700m, 2.5 hours) you are at a quite high point for this area, and surrounded by marvellous peaks: the Mweelrea massif to the west, and working rightwards from there the Sheeffrys, the Maumtrasna plateau, the Devilsmother, the Maumturks, the Twelve Bens and the Benchoonas in a 360 degree arc. Yes, this is a great eyrie and the views are just as good later on.

Head west from the cairn for less than 500m, then swing north over easy ground to a narrow col and climb directly to the south top of Ben Creggan (687m). Continue north to the next col, where there are the remains of a stone hut, and climb the north top (693m), from where the views of Mweelrea and the bland slopes of the Sheeffrys to the north are superb. From here walk east along the crest of the northern spur, passing by some impressive chasms in the ground on the initial descent, this being an area where rock predominates. As you progress the underfoot conditions become softer but the views continue to be superb. Don't be tempted to take a short cut to the road along this spur, by the way. The slope may not look too severe from the crest but much of it is blocked by cliffs farther down and later by forest in the valley.

The spur comes to an ignominious end in bogland with a corner of forest close by on the left. Roughly follow the forest edge downhill to cross a drainage channel close to the road. Once on it turn right for the nearby start.

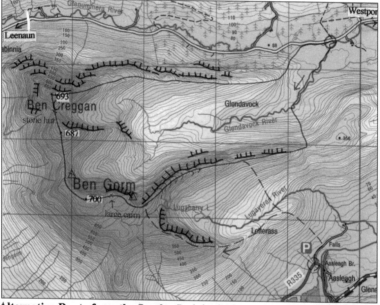

Alternative Route from the South: Park in the large carpark at Aasleagh Falls (GR 894644) less than 3 miles (4km) from Leenaun. This walk is also feasible using the 61 (express), 419 (non-summer) or 420 (summer) bus or Connemara Bus to Leenaun.

Climb to the crest of the spur to the north and then walk to Ben Gorm or Ben Creggan. Return along the spur walked on the ascent for the main route above. The walking time to Ben Creggan (the longer route) is 5 hours (distance 11km, climb 1060m). ∎

ROUTE 17: GLENINAGH CIRCUIT

If I had to choose one mountain range in Ireland in which to walk it would have to be the Twelve Bens. For challenging and exhilarating walking on steep, rocky ground it is unsurpassed. Gleninagh is the valley at the centre of a circuit which encompasses Benbaun (729m), the highest Ben of them all. A memorable walk but keep it for a fine day both for scenic and navigational reasons.

Getting There: The start is over 6 miles (10km) north of Recess at a junction of the R344 and a side road (GR 819562), the only junction for miles. At the time of writing it is inadvisable to park on the side road because of objections from the landowner. **Buses:** 61 (express, summer only, stopping at the junction at GR 8160), 419 (non-summer only equivalent of 61, but a service also runs along the R335 north of Maum Bridge), 420 (summer only, one service runs along the N59 between Leenaun and Kylemore, another along the R335 north of Maum Bridge).

Walking Time: 6.25 hours (distance 13km, climb 1240m), including 0.75 hours over Naismith for steep descents.

Difficulties: The navigational difficulty about the Twelve Bens in general, and it applies to this route, is that it is easy to navigate in good visibility since the narrow ridges are so clearly defined, but exceptionally difficult in bad because it is necessary to be able to distinguish steep, rocky slopes that are on the route from all too similar slopes *that are not and that end in sheer cliffs*. Be very careful therefore, about attempting this route in other than good conditions.

Map: Sheet 37 or the 1:50 000 'Connemara' map/guide.

Route: Walk along the side road for a few metres, turning off to the right at any convenient point to climb initially west to the indistinct top of Knockpasheemore (412m). From there continue, now south-west, towards the towering Benbaun ahead. All along here, and indeed right from the start, it is wet and soft underfoot, not at all the type of terrain associated with the Bens.

The transition from soft bogland to typical rocky Twelve Bens country takes place in a few steps and is accompanied by a sudden steepening in the slope. It is a tough but memorable haul to the summit of Benbaun (729m), though one with no navigational difficulties. Just remember in bad weather to veer left when you near the summit to reach the trig pillar (2.5 hours). What a viewpoint! Close to the centre of the Bens, with a whole array of peaks, Bens and non-Bens, jostling near at hand and reaching out into the far distance.

Head south from Benbaun to the col at Maumina (at GR 7853) - this is the more northerly of the two cols whose names are sometimes confused), on the descent veering right if you encounter crags. Maumina is wet, broad for cols in the Bens and affords an easy escape north-east into Gleninagh: there is none such on offer for the rest of the route. From Maumina ascend to the higher col just to south - this is Mám Dearg - and from there climb steeply to Bencollaghduff to the east, taking in or easily avoiding the occasional scramble on the way. Cross the plateau forming the summit of Bencollaghduff (696m) and then descend south-east to the gently-sloped red slabs at another col, Mám na bFonsaí (GR 806524).

There is no need to climb to the summit of Bencorr; instead head east from Mám na bFonsaí to Bencorr's north-west side, until you hit the narrow ridge reaching north-eastward. This is a superb section with cliffs on both sides and in particular, the rock-climbing wall of Carrot Ridge on the left.

Climb the indistinct summit 653m and descend north-west from it to yet another col before tackling Bencorrbeg (577m). Descend north on a steep but

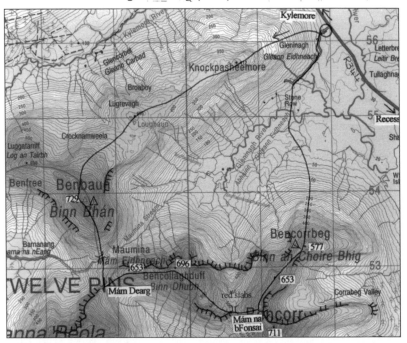

mostly grassy slope (it doesn't matter if you fail to identify Bencorrbeg and consequently continue north-east as the ground is not too steep in this direction). As you descend aim for a section of ground below reaching northwards and a little higher than the bogland of the valley. Cross this ground and the main stream of the valley. Be prepared here for wet feet or worse still, a detour up the valley in order to cross it. On its far side take a path to reach the edge of a nearby small area of forest. Walk along its side, and turn right onto a track beyond it to reach the nearby start. ∎

ROUTE 18: THE BENLETTERY HORSESHOE

One of the finest, if not the finest, mountain walk in Ireland. Not lengthy and ascending only to 711m, but the several steep and long ascents and descents make it the most challenging walk in the entire area. The magnificent setting of the Bens - bare rocky peaks rising all round - mitigate the imposition on long-suffering legs.

Getting There: Start at the youth hostel (GR 777483) on the N59 about 8 miles (13km) east of Clifden. A car left at the foot of Derryclare (at about GR 806490) will eliminate the road walk at the end of a long day. To get there, drive east from the hostel, take the first turn left after about 1 mile and park after another mile or more. **Buses:** 61 (express, summer only, stopping at Canal Bridge (GR 8047), 419 (non-summer only, along the N59).

Walking Time: 8.5 hours (distance 15km, climb 1680m) including 1.5 hours for steep descents.

Difficulties: Because of its strenuousness not a route for the faint-hearted (though an escape route is given below). In common with most of the Bens, the navigational difficulties are slight in good weather and horrendous in bad - see the comment under route 17. Good underfoot conditions nearly everywhere.

Map: Sheet 37, plus (maybe) 44 for the very south. The 1:50 000 'Connemara' map/guide covers the entire route.

Route: Climb Benlettery (577m) directly from the hostel, an unrelenting climb and soggy underfoot for much of the way, to be rewarded at the top by marvellous views of the Bens and a lake-studded bogland to the south.

From here on, the characteristic rocky terrain of the Bens predominates and progress is that much easier. Walk directly to nearby Bengower (664m), taking care not to confuse the prominent cairn marking the point of departure to Benglenisky for the summit of Bengower. (This cairn is important for the short variation below.)

From Bengower descend steeply northwards to a narrow col and climb through avoidable scree, the only sustained scree on or near the entire route, to the summit of Benbreen (691m). Benbreen is the only mountain with some navigational difficulties even in good visibility. Follow the summit plateau north-west for about 500m and then swing north-east (not east onto the wrong spur) with cliffs close on the left. This north-east spur takes you down to the col at GR 788527 (4.5 hours), Mám Dearg.

This is a magical eyrie. Right at the centre of the Bens and with towering peaks in all directions, it is a great place to marvel at the majesty of this superb range and (more prosaically) a good place for a break. It is also possible to retreat south-east from here into lower ground. If you do, head directly for the nearest road as the valley bottom is exceptionally wet.

There is a steep climb eastward to Bencollaghduff (696m), followed by a descent over broad, gently-sloping red slabs to the pass of Mám na bhFonsaí (GR 806524). From here there is yet another steep climb to Bencorr (711m), the highest peak of the day. Beyond it is the last climb, not as severe as those already done, but no pushover either at this late stage. This is to Derryclare (over

44 Connemara & the Burren

670m), on the way to which you pass a tiny lake and the remains of a stone shelter.

The descent from Derryclare is not altogether straightforward. To avoid cliffs to the right you must descend south for about 1.5km before venturing right to meet the track. This stretch is boggy with an intermittent path, which is some help in navigation. Once on the track turn left, and right onto the N59 to reach the hostel, thus making a total of 4km on road or track.

Easier Variation: This will give you some idea of the Bens, without the heroic exertions of the main route. Take the main route to Bengower, retrace steps to the cairn at the turn-off to Benglenisky (516m) and walk west to the mountain. Continue west downhill, following the forest on the left. Turn left on tarmac and left again onto the N59, thus leaving nearly 3km back to the hostel. Total walking time is 4 hours (distance 11km, climb 700m). ∎

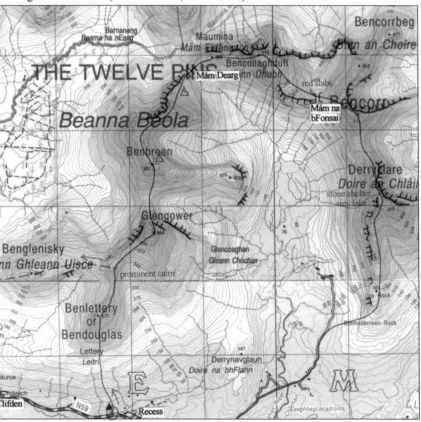

ROUTE 19: THE FAILMORE CIRCUIT

A range of great character and interest, the Maumturks are essentially a plateau, though it doesn't seem like one when you are negotiating its rock-strewn fastnesses. This route, through quintessential Maumturks, covers the part of the range between two of the passes that sever the range and takes in the highest peak, a modest 702m.

Getting There: From Maum Bridge, take the road towards Maum Cross, turn first right, turn left after 1.9 miles, and drive another 1 mile to park just before a bridge; there is plenty of room for cars (GR 925524). As you approach the bridge look out on the right for a gate you can use at the end of the walk. **Buses:** 61 (express to Maum Cross), 419 (non-summer only), 420 (summer only) both to Maum Bridge.

Walking Time: 5.5 hours (distance 13km, climb 840m) including 0.5 hours over Naismith for one steep descent.

Difficulties: Navigation is the big problem in bad weather, with the entire high plateau requiring quite a convoluted course. The landmarks noted below are quite difficult to recognise when you need them most. If you are completely lost head south-west to avoid cliffs to the north-east.

Map: The 1:50 000 'Connemara' map/guide covers the whole route adequately. Sheet 37 does not cover some of the lowland section so you may like to supplement it with sheet 38.

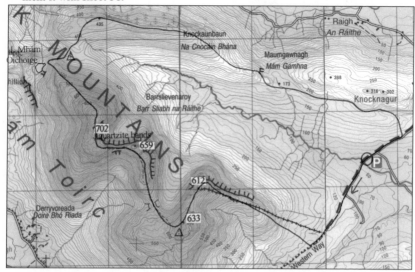

Route: Walk onward on a track from the bridge, keeping to the Western Way where the track swings left. Walk steadily uphill for over 10 minutes to cross a gate and here turn right to follow a fence which heads west uphill and indeed will do so all the way to near the summit of Binn Mhairg (612m). If you care to cross the fence some way up on this steady ascent you will find yourself on the edge of a line of high cliffs overlooking the Failmore River and the spur beyond the river on which you end this walk.

If you haven't already done so, veer away from the right of this fence where it takes two right-angle bends. Here the ground has begun to level off and it is only a short walk to the summit. Like all summits in the Maumturks, it's unimpressive. What *is* impressive though is the sweep of cliff falling northward to bogland and westward to a high rocky corrie. There's much more of this magnificent terrain later!

Nearby Binn Caonaigh (633m) to the south, the next summit on the route, barely rises from the general level, though the views from it and its setting are marvellous. In bad weather don't try to find the highest point among the rocky hummocks and lochans scattered hereabouts; instead make for the col to the north-west (at GR 896517) which carries, would you believe, a path through the shattered quartzite stones. Beyond the col climb about 100m to the next section of the Maumturks plateau, the one rising to Binn idir an Dá Log (702m), the highest point in the entire range.

To reach it requires a zig-zag course, navigation helped by a path which runs to the west of the Maumturk's rocky crest. The only other navigational aid are the long (tens of metres) bands of white quartzite running across the face of Binn idir an Dá Log, that just before the summit cairn being particularly broad.

From the summit (2.75 hours) take a general bearing somewhat to the right of Lough Mhám Oichóige (GR 8853) as the direct descent will take you over crags. This circular lake (3.5 hours) is in a lovely location somewhat above the major col that gashes the centre of the 'Turks. From here there's a tricky bit of navigation. Contour roughly east and then north-east from the lake for 400m or so, guided by a fence, then head north up a steep grassy slope (from here on you are out of rocky terrain) and so gain Knocknagur, a spur which runs eastward for over 4km.

The rest is easy. Follow the high ground for over 2km at the end of which make a steep descent enlivened by unexpected crags. At lower ground contour onwards with high rocky ground now close on the left. This should take you through a tiny, flat, grassy valley, hemmed in by moorland on the right and crags on the left. Bear right at its end and carefully cross fences to reach a gate leading onto the road. Turn right for the nearby start.

Easy Variation: With two cars or, only if you are staying in Clifden, with fortuituous connections on the 419 and 61 (express stopping at Recess) buses, you can walk the Western Way on track. This takes you right through the Maumturks, and gives you a good idea of its character. With two cars, start in the same place as the main route and simply follow the Way to tarmac. To get a car to the finish take the N59 towards Galway, turning right at the signpost for Mamean. Turn left at the tee (the right branch is a track) and park a little further on at an rough carpark (GR 892495). Walking time is about 1.5 hours (distance 5km, climb 200m). The bus variation, which starts at Maum Bridge, is much longer and involves much walking on country roads (4 hours, distance 16km, climb 200m). ∎

Much more grassy than the rest of the Maumturks - and indeed plain boggy in parts - this is a fairly gentle route for the area. From the tops there are great views encompassing a complex interplay of inlet, sea and mountain. Indeed, even the initial lowland stretch, a part of the Western Way, is highly scenic.

Getting There: Start in the village of Leenaun (GR 8761). **Buses:** 61 (express, summer), 419 (non-summer) 420 (summer) (all to Leenaun).

Walking Time: 4.5 hours (distance 12km, climb 700m) with some easy track walking compensating for one steep descent.

Difficulties: Some boggy ground underfoot. Navigation generally not all that easy especially in bad visibility, though mistakes should not be disastrous. Take care to avoid rocky crags on the steep descent from Leenaun Hill.

Map: Sheet 37 or the 1:50 000 'Connemara' map/guide.

Route: Take the N59 (it's also the Western Way) towards Clifden, keeping with the Way by bearing left onto a track after over 1km. Follow it gently uphill and then gently downhill for about another 3km until you reach tarmac at the entrance to the long wooded forest occupying Glengraff. Turn left here and continue straight ahead where the Western Way turns right. The next kilometre or so is in forest but it is not all coniferous and the occasional clump of deciduous trees as well as the odd house, deserted or occupied, make the going pleasant, as well as undemanding.

When you finally emerge from forest you are at the last house in the valley. Turn left just before it to take a rough path round the house and across a stream, a tributary of the Bunowen River, the main stream in Glengraff. Here at long last you face a climb, the only sustained one of the day. As you ascend roughly eastward following the stream you have just crossed, you will observe that it has cut a spectacular gully into the soft sloping bogland. You might also note the grassy low point in the Maumturks less than 2 kilometres off to the south-east. Low point is apt in both senses, since this marks the point where weary walkers on the infamous Maumturks walk face their last climb, one of 350m. Since they have already climbed over 2000m, it is no wonder that this particular low point is sometimes called the col of despondency!

Our more modest climb comes to an end on the edge of a grassy plateau at the undistinguished point 578m with a curve of mountain reaching round to north and to south-east, whither we are headed. From here to Leenaun Hill less than 2km away there is an undulating march through occasional peat hags Apart from excellent views of the rest of the Maumturks to the south, the rocky haystack-like peaks of the Bens to the south-west and the Mweelrea massif to the north-west there is also a most impressive corrie close by to the north, whose lip steepens here and there into crags. It is hard to think of many areas in Ireland around which rise so many diverse ranges. With all this splendour in view you can follow a fence all the way to Leenaun Hill (618m).

From here take the narrow spur to the north, thus heading, as you will see when you get within range, back to the village of Leenaun. At any convenient point come right off the spur to reach a shallow valley close to the Leenaun to Maum

Bridge road. As you descend about east you might note the landform on the far side of the main stream in the valley. Here the land rises steeply in two distinct terraces to a plateau. These terraces mark the shorelines of ancient lakes held back by an ice dam further down the valley.

The walk along the valley is delightful: its stream plunges here and there in short but impressive waterfalls terminated by deep pools. Cross the stream at any convenient point to reach a track onto which you turn left downhill to reach tarmac. Turn left to reach nearby Leenaun. ■

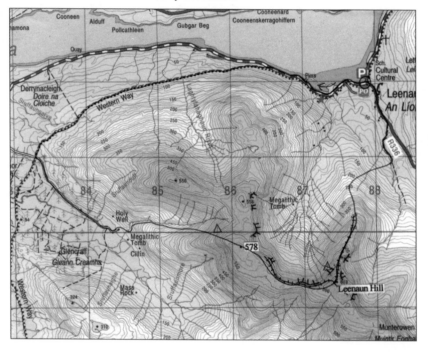

The Benchoonas, wedged between Killary Harbour and the far larger Twelve Bens are a small and most attractive range, a tangle of rocky mountain and lochan-scattered plateau. It's a good area for improvising as the mood takes you and as the weather changes.

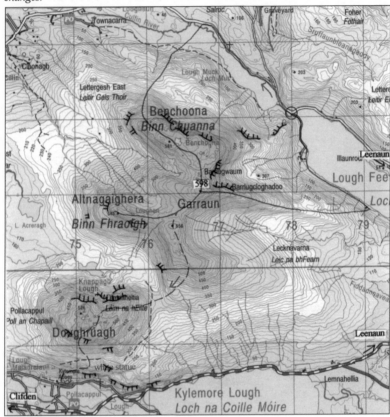

Getting There: From *Leenaun* drive west for 4.5 miles (7km) along the N59, here take the second of two closely spaced turns on the right (among many others, there's a small black and yellow sign here stating N59 1204). From *Kylemore* take the second turn left after the junction of the R344. In both cases drive the length of Lough Fee and park near the bridge over the exit stream from that lake (GR 780620). This route is ideal if you are staying at Little Killary youth hostel. **Buses:** 61 (express, summer only, to junction at GR 8160), 419 (non-summer only equivalent of 61), 420 (summer only, one service runs along the N59, another between the junction at GR 8160 and Lettergesh (GR 7563)).

Walking Time: 3.75 hours (distance 10km, climb 600m).

Difficulties: Although there is wet ground in the lowlands and short stretches of cliff in the area, the route is not difficult, either underfoot or navigationally.

Map: Sheet 37 or 1:50 000 'Connemara' map/guide.

Route: Walk north-west along the road, traverse the length of Lough Muck and pass a small church. A few hundred metres beyond it cross the river on the left by a concrete bridge that has collapsed in the middle, the second of two shaky crossing points. Head south-west to cross bogland, and at the first point where the crags on the north side of Benchoona look easily negotiable, climb south to gain the summit ridge.

Once on the crest of the ridge walk uphill roughly south-east to the summit, or rather to the western end of the summit plateau (581m). On this longish ascent you will want to catch your breath - and admire the scenery. That oceanward to a scattering of islands, of which the block of Clare Island to the north is the largest, is particularly noteworthy. From the two closely-spaced cairns on Benchoona's western end head east among the peat hags, small lakes and rocky knolls of the summit plateau, and at its end, and here in bad visibility cliffs will rudely halt your onward advance, swing south to drop to a high col facing Garraun and then climb to its summit.

Garraun (598m) is quite a contrast to Benchoona, being a grassy, soft mound. It hardly needs saying that the views from it, particularly towards the Bens to the south, are magnificent. There are several route choices from this summit. You can head for home along its eastern spur, you can carry on to Doughruagh if you are on the A to B route (see below) or you can do a there-and-back to Altnagaighera (543m) to the west, this latter being the main route. Altnagaighera is only a grassy, hummocky spur but the strange conglomerate rocks scattered along its crest, as well as the views south down to Knappagh Lough make it well worth the effort. From the end of the spur, marked by a steep drop and crags ahead, return to the summit of Garraun and walk down the eastern spur.

This spur is narrow and most distinct so it should be easy to keep to its crest. The view north to and over Lough Fee is magnificent, that south over a wide dull valley less so. Keep to the crest until you near Lough Fee and then veer left off it to reach its shore close to a house on a delta. Turn left to walk along the shore and when you come close to a new plantation keep on the lakeshore to avoid it and to respect the privacy of the residents of houses here. Just beyond these houses you will reach a track which will take you the short distance back to the start.

A to B Variation: A more varied version of the main route but with transport problems unless you have two cars, one of which should be left at Kylemore Abbey on the N59 (GR 7458). Take the main route to the summit of Garraun and then walk south-west over pt 556m. Descend to the col to the east of Doughruagh and then climb to the summit plateau, which is similar to Benchoona, though more rocky. Now the difficult bit: descend through crags and steep ground to a white statue, which is necessary to find to avoid thick rhododendron further down. At the statue turn right onto a path heading down to the Abbey. Total walking time 4.25 hours (distance 9km, climb 880m) including about 15 minutes over Naismith for the steep descent at the end. ■

ROUTE 22: BLACK HEAD

From afar, great gently contorted piles of grey plates, the largest at the bottom; on the walk, platforms of deeply fissured limestone, each platform terminated by a short cliff. In an overused word the Burren is unique. Not really a hill-walking area, since the highest point rises to only 344m, yet for its geological and botanical interest, the Burren is well worth a leisurely walk.

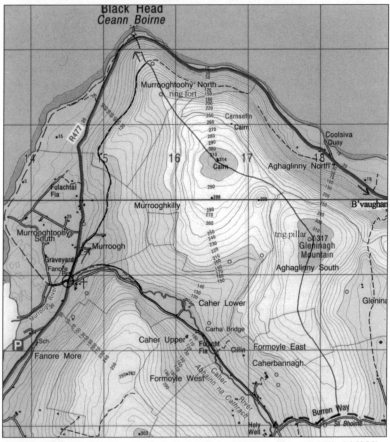

Getting There: Start at the junction off the R477 in Fanore (GR 146089). Fanore is hard to pin down, but this junction is easy to find, as there is a prominent church on the side road. **Bus:** 423 along the R477 via Fanore Cross.

Walking Time: 4.5 hours (distance 15km, climb 360m), though this is not an area where you can, or will want to set a world walking record.

Difficulties: Watch out that you do not crock your ankle as you walk across the platforms. The higher off-road sections require a little navigational care, as the Burren plateau is a little featureless. However mistakes should not be serious.

Map: Sheet 51. You might also like to invest in Tim Robinson's map 'The Burren' for the wealth of archaeological and other detail it gives.

Route: From the junction walk north along the main road, the R477, and take the first gravel road on the right after about 300m. Walk up this road for about 5 minutes, at which point it swings sharply right at a house on that side. Leave it here by crossing the wall ahead and walking an indistinct path beyond.

After a few anxious minutes the path metamorphoses into a clear, wide, grassy track between high stone walls, that pursues a leisurely incline across the side of Black Head. Along here, among other delights, the Aran Islands off to the west and the hummocky Twelve Bens and plateau-like Maumturks to the north-west across Galway Bay are revealed. Continue the gentle climb for about an hour from the start of the route; here the track has begun to swing right from its hitherto north-east course and a lighthouse is directly below you, though you will have to walk downhill a little to see it. At about here, the exact point is not critical, it is time to decide whether you are going to walk the main route or the variation.

If you want to do the main route, climb directly past a most impressive ring fort and, now walking on the typical Burren terrain of pavement and cliff continue south-east to pt 314m, which is crowned by an impressive cairn. You are now on some of the highest ground of the Burren and the views to other sections of this high ground, to east and south, are quite unforgettable, an austere moon-like landscape of grey layered limestone.

The next target is Gleninagh Mountain off to the south-east. The way there is straightforward, across a limestone ridge to the left of a grassy circular depression marked as 205m on the map (which makes it look like a summit), from where there is a short climb to the stubby trig pillar.

The plateau is fairly indistinct, so don't assume you know the direction from Gleninagh; head initially south-west keeping to the higher ground, so passing occasional patches of rich grass among the pavements. You should also cross a slightly elevated mound of such grass, crowned by a cairn. Beyond it continue south heading for a track, the route of the Burren Way. You should reach it at about its highest point and turn right.

Turn right again at nearby tarmac and walk the last 4km downhill, through a valley of upland farmland and scrubby bushes yielding to limestone higher up the hillsides. However, just for variety, you can walk the last kilometre on an intermittent track. You will see a point where there are metal poles spanning the river on the right. Cross here and initially walk the bank above the river and further down walk through fields to reach the R477.

Short Variation: This is a lovely route, mostly by the sea and in spite of its proximity to the road, with a remote atmosphere. From Black Head on the main route (see above) walk directly downhill to the road, cross it at about the lighthouse and turn left. A varied terrain follows: a short section of sea-cliff, limestone pavements, a storm beach, tiny rising fields on the left. When you reach sand dunes you can turn inland and so reach the R477 at about the starting point. The total walking time is 2 hours (distance 7km, climb 140m). ■

ROUTE 23: BRANDON

A classic! From the initial ascent up rocky slopes, each ending at a mountain lochan nestling between progressively closer and mightier cliffs, to the summit of Brandon Mountain itself (952m) and the subsequent walk along the jagged edge of the Brandon massif, each step of the way reveals new delights. A long, arduous but highly rewarding walk. Don't forget that the variations are much shorter.

Getting There: The start is about 25 miles (40km) from Tralee. Follow the N86 initially, continue straight ahead on the R560 where the N86 swings left, and then follow signs for Cloghane (Clochán). Just before the village cross a bridge, pass the Garda (police) station on the right immediately beyond it, cross another bridge and take the next left. Drive for 2.0 miles to cross two adjacent bridges (GR 490084). Park anywhere on the road side after them. If you have a second car leave it near the end of the road (GR 471068) to avoid a road walk of nearly 3km at the end. **Bus:** 273 (Friday only to Cloghane).

Walking Time: 7 hours (distance 17km, climb 1140m), including a half-hour over Naismith for the initial rough terrain. This includes the road walk.

Difficulties: Easy navigation and mostly good underfoot conditions.

Map: Sheet 70. It shows only a small section of the path from Faha (see below) and forest far higher on the eastern side of Brandon than in reality.

Route: Take the track running west between the two bridges, walk to the farmhouse and ask permission of the friendly people there to continue. Walk up the track for a few hundred metres, noting ahead the fine corrie from which a waterfall gushes. That's not the way you're going! Instead, watch out for a stream descending from your right and at any convenient point head towards it and follow it upstream, crossing fences carefully. It doesn't matter which bank you walk but you are aiming for the north-east side of the lakes ahead. However even if you elect to walk the western bank you can cross the causeway at Loch Cruite, the first of the lakes in the paternoster string.

This lake is the largest of all on the route. What a location: a long, jagged line of cliffs on its south-west side and the great corrie climbing skyward to the north-west. And this is only the first of several equally scenic lakes.

There's a steep but short climb to the next lake, Lough Nalacken, and an equally short but steeper climb over sloping slabs to the next. This climb is best undertaken with the waterfall, one of several on this stretch, on your right. After which little need be said, as you will be channelled along the boulder-strewn bottom of the narrowing corrie. As for the scenery and the ambience: it's stupendous!

Near the end of the corrie you will notice the path from Faha marching gently down the grassy slope on the right. You will eventually join it in a comparatively level area where there are several lakes tucked into rocky basins. From here on follow the path which climbs the corrie wall and which, in spite of its steepness, should not cause vertigo.

This path ends abruptly at the top of the cliffs. Turn left here to walk a few hundred metres (distance) and 70m or so (climb) to the trig pillar, just one of the

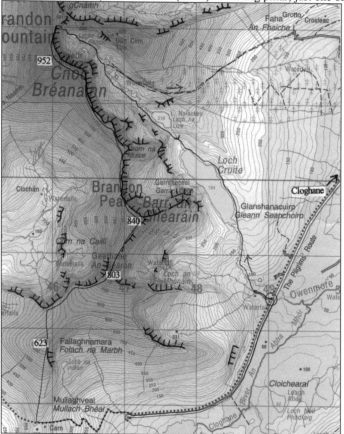

items on the summit of Brandon Mountain (952m, 4 hours). From the summit, the highest point in Ireland outside the Reeks, you can see the great line of cliffs reaching to north and south, the mountains of the rest of the peninsula to the east and in stark contrast, a comparatively gentle moorland, ending at a line of sea-cliffs to north-west and west, beyond which are a scattering of islands of which Great Blasket is the largest and the Skelligs the most distinctive. At least, I hope you see all this, because the summit is frequently shrouded in cloud: as they say in these parts, 'it wears its cap'. If visibility is good, you could hardly hope for a more majestic scene, one that you will enjoy from varying angles all the way along the cliff edge.

The next goal is Brandon Peak. Walk south-east from the summit with the cliffs on the left. Navigationally this is easy: there are two comparatively minor tops on the generally downward trend. You don't have to climb them - but don't mistake them for Brandon Peak (840m) itself, which is preceded by a sustained climb of 90m (the other two climbs are not more than 30m each).

From Brandon Peak walk south to Gearhane (803m). While the cliffs ease on this stretch there is still a narrow but grassy, not quite knife-edge ridge just before the summit which might be a useful indication of your position in bad visibility. Just south of Gearhane is a strange sight for this height: a gate with accompanying fences. Keep to the right of these to walk along the edge of cliffs facing north-west towards the ocean.

After about 1km from the summit of Gearhane the cliffs swing to north-facing. Here you must leave them and make your way south over gently sloping bogland. Climb the short distance to pt 623m, which overlooks a half-hearted corrie holding Loch na mBan. About 1km south of it, at a shallow col and close to a great line of mighty cliffs to the south-east, you will meet the waymarked Pilgrims' Route.

The rest is easy: turn left onto the Route and take it down to the end of a road in the remote end of the valley where you started. From here, assuming no car, you will have another 3km of weary walk. One word of consolation: you will soon get over tired legs but, with a bit of luck, you will have memories that will last a lifetime.

Shorter Variation: Take the main route to the meeting with the Faha path, and follow this path all the way back to Faha (GR 493119). This gives you a good idea of the majestic scenery in the area without having an over-strenuous climb. It means two cars or a pleasant 6km road walk at the end. Total walking time is 4.25 hours (distance 13km, climb 460m) including the road walk.

Much Shorter Variation: Walk at least as far as the first lake, Loch Cruite, taking in Loch an Mhónáin on the way. You will see the waterfall issuing from this lake shortly after you have passed the farmhouse. ■

Beenkeragh (Route 25)

ROUTE 24: CIRCUIT OF GLANTEENASSIG

A gradual climb up the rock-strewn eastern shoulder of Stradbally Mountain (798m), with its great red sandstone cliffs and buttresses increasingly dominant. The descent follows the tops of the cliffs wooded Glanteenassig and its sub-valleys, before descending to Lough Slat. A varied and not too demanding walk.

Getting There: From Tralee (16 miles (26km) away) take the N86 and then the R560 where the N86 swings left, keep straight ahead again where the R560 swings right to Castlegregory, then take the next turn left after only a few hundred metres (signposted 'Glass Studio'). Drive 1.3 miles to park carefully on the verge (GR 618099). **Bus:** 273 to the junction on the R560 at GR 6211.

Walking Time: 5.5 hours (distance 14km, climb 980m). There are several opportunities, both easier and harder, to vary this.

Difficulties: Easy underfoot and navigationally, except on the last descent where attention to navigation is necessary.

Map: Sheets 70 and 71. Both sheets show forest well in excess of reality.

Route: From the start, as well as picking out much of the circuit, you will see close at hand to the south-west the spur cradling Arraglen Lake. Climb to its rocky crest and clamber along it; for easier walking you might like to keep to Arraglen Lake's shore or on the right of the crest, where you can enjoy lovely views around the corrie holding the lake.

After a short distance the slope eases and a long, steady climb westward to the summit of Stradbally Mountain ensues. As you advance the cliffs on the left become more formidable, though not as formidable as those off to the south of Stradbally. Here massive, almost vertical slabs, a mighty buttress and scree spilling downwards towards the wooded shores of Lough Cam far below make a dramatic scene.

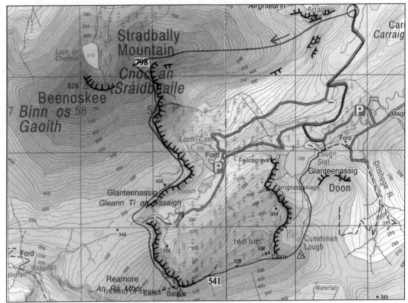

An increasing number of rocks heralds the summit of Stradbally Mountair (798m). In fact the summit itself, crowned by a huge cairn, is a boulder field. The forest shown on sheet 70 reaching to the summit is nowhere near it, which is just as well because the views from here, close to the centre of the peninsula, are magnificent, and only a little blocked by Stradbally's twin, nearby Beenoskee.

If you are into peak-bagging you might like to climb Beenoskee (826m), whose summit is obvious because of its toppled trig pillar (this addition is not included above in the walking time). If you do make sure you reach the next section of cliff south of Stradbally as high on the shoulder of that mountain as possible; otherwise you will miss some of the best scenery.

From Stradbally walk south-east to the nearby cliffs and simply follow them down. A lovely section, giving new angles on the cliffs and down into the woods and lakes of Glanteenassig, the centre-piece of the walk.

After nearly 2km from the summit of Stradbally, the slope eases and the cliff edge swings decisively from south-east to south-west. Beyond this, where the cliff swings back to west, you may like to avail of an escape route (at 3 hours' walking time). Watch out where forest creeps up what is now merely steep ground on the left. Here you can clamber down the grassy slope to the valley floor and then follow a stream to the nearby forest track.

If however you wish to do the whole route, continue along the cliff edge, noting as you once again reach nearly level ground a huge mound of stones off to the right, locally known as Cu Chulainn's house.

Navigation is now the main priority. In bad weather, simply walk along the cliff edge until it swings north-east and then follow a compass bearing of 77° for 2km - this should take you to the spur just south of Cumminan Lough (see below). In good weather you can afford to follow a line of red stones along the crest of the spur. This is not part of an old roadway; instead, more prosaically it is a firebreak, though in spite of the map's assertion otherwise, the nearest forest is a long way down the slope. Follow this firebreak round to the north-east to pt 541m. Beyond it, where the firebreak descends to the left, keep to the crest of a now broad ridge.

There are two prominent tors (heaps of rocks) to the north of the rounded summit of pt 552m that might help you to identify it. To avoid cliffs to the east of the summit you should steer well to its south so as to walk to just south of Cumminan Lough and then turn directly to the lough itself.

Navigational troubles now behind, walk north to descend a fairly steep, grassy slope to the shores of Lough Slat. It's a lovely location: the large lake set in an isolated bowl, a partly wooded lakeside and high, frowning slabs of cliff soaring above to west and south-east.

A complicated set of directions now follows that take you only a few hundred metres. Please bear with me and don't quote it as typical of my writing style!

Turn right when you reach the lakeshore and right again away from the lake at a high stone wall, which ends only 100m or so from the lake at a gate. Cross this gate to reach a path bordering forest and turn right onto it. Cross the first gate on the left into forest and ford the river. Walk to a track and turn left. Walk to a tee and turn right. Now simply keep to this one and only track until you are out of forest. Turn right onto a minor road and walk less than 2km to the start. ■

ROUTE 25: THE BEENKERAGH RIDGE

There are many lovely walks to be had taking in Carrauntoohil so it is hard to pick one. This route is a moderately short but tough walk which takes in the three highest peaks in Ireland, passing from Carrauntoohil (1039m) to Beenkeragh (1010m) along the finest (and most vertigo-inducing) ridge walk in Ireland, the Beenkeragh Ridge. Predictably marvellous views. All in all, a classic, but if you suffer from vertigo, try the alternative route given here.

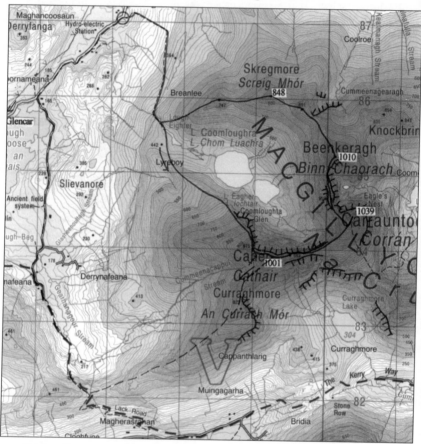

Getting There: In Killorglin take the road signposted 'Glencar 15km', swing right with the main road after 0.7 miles, keep straight ahead after another 4.4 miles and park carefully 1.2 miles farther on at double gates on the left (GR 772870). You can also reach this point from Killarney (20 miles, 32km via Killorglin) or from nearby Glencar.

Walking (and Scrambling) Time: 6.75 hours, including about one hour for scrambling (distance 12km, climb 1260m).

Difficulties: The exposure on the Beenkeragh Ridge has already been mentioned. If you walk the route in the anti-clockwise direction as suggested here, you will face the worst part of the Ridge first and so can retreat if needs be, having declined the challenge, but with Carrauntoohil climbed. Navigation is easy and underfoot conditions good.

Map: Sheet 78 or the 1:25 000 "Macgillycuddy's Reeks" map, which far better shows the Beenkeragh Ridge.

Route: From the gates follow the track all the way to its end at a dam at the western end of Lough Eighter. The dull stretch now behind, walk south to reach a long spur heading towards the summit of Caher, and on the spur's crest turn south-east to follow an increasingly clear path upward to Caher, the huge cliffs overlooking Lough Eagher increasingly imposing on the left.

Caher (1001m) is in effect a long, narrow, grassy ridge, with three summits (the transverse fence between the first and second maybe some help in bad visibility). From the third summit, there is a steep drop before the final climb to Carrauntoohil itself. At 1039m, Carrauntoohil (3.5 hours) is the highest mountain in Ireland and has a fitting location. A blunt wedge pointing north, it is faced on the north and east by formidable cliffs, while to the north-east runs the jagged Beenkeragh Ridge, which we must now seriously consider.

It is most important to retrace steps about 100m south-west from the summit so as to face the ridge squarely; it initially runs north-west. That done you have to find your way along the narrow rocky ground where, as already said, the most 'airy' part comes early on, after a col south of Cumeenoughter Lake (GR 8084). To avoid the worst, look out for traces of a path on the left (west) of the crest.

The definitive end of the Ridge is heralded by a steep rock-strewn ascent to Beenkeragh (1010m), from where take the north-west (not north-east) ridge on an exhilarating jaunt over the three main summits of Skregmore. The end of the Skregmore summits is obvious: there is a steep descent west to Lough Eighter. From here pick up the outward track back to the start.

A Shorter Variation: *This route takes in Caher and Carrauntoohil but not the Beenkeragh Ridge; it is thus suitable if you suffer from vertigo or if the weather is bad. You can postpone a decision on which route to take until you reach the summit of Carrauntoohil. Though without the excitement of the main route this variation is otherwise almost as enjoyable.*

Route: Take the main route to the summit of Carrauntoohil, noting on the way the second (1001m) summit of Caher, which, as you see above, is just after the transverse fence and is important for the return. From Carrauntoohil (3.5 hours) return by the same route to Caher (1001m). From here walk the spur to the south-west taking in Curraghmore, which has no discernible rise, and from it continue along a more indistinct and rough spur heading for the highest point of the pass through which the Kerry Way (aka the Lack Road) runs. Turn right onto it and follow it all the way back to tarmac near Lough Acoose. Turn right here and walk 1.5km to the start. The total walking time is 6.5 hours (distance 17km, climb 1120m). ∎

A steep and direct approach to the spectacular Reeks Ridge, whose great cliffs overlook corrie lakes and beyond them the plains of Kerry. With much of the narrow, rocky arête over 900m, rising to 988m at Cnoc na Péiste, this is no place for the faint-hearted, but if you are prepared for a hard walk you will undoubtedly have an exciting day.

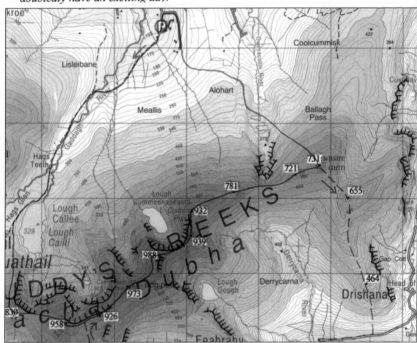

Getting There: From *Killarney* drive to Beaufort, here take the road which skirts the northern side of the Reeks, turning left just after Kissane's shop at the sign 'Carrauntoohil 4'. Drive to the carpark at the end of the road (GR 837873), where there is a small charge. From *Killorglin* take the road signposted 'Glencar 15km' in the town, keeping straight ahead after 0.7 miles and right at the sign 'Carrauntoohil 4'.

Walking Time: 6.5 hours (distance 15km, climb 1300m), allowing about a half-hour extra for slow going over an exposed terrain on the Ridge. Surprisingly (see below), there are several options to shorten the route.

Difficulties: Vertigo may be a problem for about 1km where the ridge is narrow, rocky and steep-sided. Navigational problems are minor.

Map: 1:25 000 "Macgillycuddy's Reeks", which clearly shows the cliffs and steep ground on each side of the Ridge, is more useful than sheet 78.

Route: From the carpark take the well-worn path into the Hag's Glen, keeping to the route indicated by arrows. This will mean fording two streams before reaching a track. From near the start the great pyramid of Carrauntoohil becomes increasingly prominent while, much nearer, you cannot mistake the great stump known as the Hag's Tooth (Teeth on the maps, though the other molars are minor and prior to the obvious one).

Rather than climb the eroded Devil's Ladder, I suggest you follow the track as far as Lough Callee, a large and therefore unmistakable lake, and then veer left away from it to climb the grassy slope ending in the eastern summit of Cnoc na Toinne (about 830m, 2.5 hours). If you have any doubt about your location the fence you cross above the col to its east will be reassuring.

A word about the scenery. From Cnoc na Toinne on, as far as the descent from the Ridge at its eastern end, the views are majestic. Apart from the long-distance panorama there are mighty cliffs at your feet with rocky spur and corrie lake, particularly to the north, providing a constantly changing interest.

Anyway, from the col east of Cnoc na Toinne climb to Cnoc na Chuillinn (958m) and with the cliffs always close on the left continue to Maolán Buí (973m), whose summit has a solitary iron post, a useful landmark since there is no other for miles around. From here walk onwards to nearby Cnoc na Péiste (988m).

So far, so vertigo-free. The next section, the kilometre from here over the Big Gun (939m) and thence on the left-ward swing to Cruach Mhór (932m) involves scrambling and requires care and time. Conventional wisdom suggests that you keep to the right on the first section as far as the Big Gun (939m) and to the left thereafter, but you will have to pick a route for yourself, using vestigial paths here and there. It may be some consolation to know that there is a prominent man-made block of stones on Cruach Mhór so that the end of the exposed section is clearly visible from afar.

The block of stones on Cruach Mhór, which is about 3m high (the block, not the mountain), turns out to be a grotto and contains a tiny statue: a bit disproportionate. From the summit descend east along the rocky, narrow ridge, mercifully with the fear of vertigo now behind. After passing the narrow col to the south of Loch an Chaca, the ridge broadens and assumes a less threatening aspect and it is an easy climb to Cnoc an Bhráca (731m), which is crowned by a fine cairn of square cross-section.

Time to start for home. Head north-west down from the cairn veering right if the slope is too steep (it shouldn't be). As you descend watch out for two lakes in the valley below and cross soft ground just to the north of the more northerly one, so heading to the crest of a long spur of high land (an esker?) reaching north. Continue on the crest for a while and as this spur merges into a broader spur of land ending in upland fields get to the crest of this latter spur (all this is not as complicated as it seems).

This route will lead you towards stone walls bordering upland fields. Close to them turn left (west) to follow a water channel which ends at the conjunction of two streams. Cross a fence and nearby gate here and so reach a track just to the north. Take it to its end and turn left for the nearby start.

Variation from the Black Valley: From the hostel (GR 8682) take the Kerry Way west, walk through a forest and, still on the Way and having just reached a road (1.25 hours) climb directly north to the crest of the Reeks Ridge. You should reach it just to the east of Cnoc na Chuillinn (958m) and can follow the main route to Cnoc an Bhráca (731m). Turn south-west from the summit to climb nearby Cnoc an dTarbh (655m), which has a heap of boulders on its summit, and continue south over rough country to Drisean (464m), which you may climb without realising it, so insignificant is the rise to the summit. Descend directly south from Drisean, climbing fences with care. Turn right when you reach the road - do not head across country - and walk the short distance to the hostel. Walking time is about 7 hours (distance 17km, climb 1250m), allowing about a half-hour extra for slow going over exposed terrain on the Ridge.

Escape Routes: Allowing for inevitable personal interpretations the map here indicates cliffs accurately. You can see from it that you can retreat cautiously from several places, northwards or easier, southwards. Though fairly prone to vertigo, I have retreated south from the Big Gun, where the contours seem to be alarmingly close together, without too much bother. ■

ROUTE 27: BENNAUNMORE

A small, quite low area (Crohane at 656m is by far the highest peak on the route) but one of constantly changing atmosphere and with a wealth of small-scale features some a legacy of volcanic activity. Essentially this an area for leisurely pottering: or at least slow pottering, given the difficult terrain underfoot.

Getting There: The start is 8 miles (13km) from Killarney. Take the N71, turn left off it after about 2½ miles (4km) just after Muckross Park Hotel - the turn is signposted 'Mangerton 2¾'. Continue straight ahead for about 4 miles (6.5km), for much of the last mile or so with Lough Guitane in the middle distance on the right. Immediately after the lake turn next right (it's narrow and has gate pillars). Drive a further 0.7 miles and park just after a farmhouse on the right, where there is a linear quarry on the left (GR 036846). This point may also be easily reached from the N22. **Buses:** 44 (express), 270, both to Glenflesk (GR 0685).

Walking Time: 4.75 hours, thus allowing about 1 hour for difficult underfoot conditions (distance 10km, climb 720m).

Difficulties: Much treacherous ground; some careful navigation needed.

Map: Sheet 79. The track onto Crohane extends much higher than shown.

Route: The first few hundred metres are the worst in the whole route, so let's get them over with. Climb the rough ground on the left of the road and continue upward heading east, praying that you will soon meet a track. This is extremely difficult ground with high vegetation and low rocks, just great for crocking an ankle. As you climb the going gets easier, but still you will no doubt be relieved to reach the track and turn right onto it to face Crohane.

The track winds upward to flat ground on Crohane's northern spur, giving widening views of the rugged area to the west and of the well-named Paps off to the east. The end of the track still means a stiff climb to the eastern summit and then a short walk to the north-facing crags at the summit itself (656m, 2 hours).

The descent from Crohane requires careful navigation as the country to the south-west is rough with no distinct features. First walk south, then veer west to climb pt 477m. The next target is the northern end of Lough Nabroda, which requires a careful descent because of steep ground and the occasional rocky outcrop. As you descend you can study the great columns of rock on the eastern side of Bennaunmore, evidence of its volcanic origin.

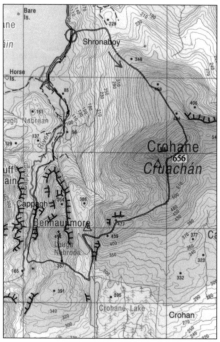

Lough Nabroda is in a dramatic location, steeply rising ground close by to east and west accentuating its remoteness. Incidentally there is no evident outlet stream - it runs underground through huge boulders on the lake's northern end. The lakeshore is an excellent place for a rest, after which you should take a path south along the lake's eastern side. Where it expires continue to the northern end of Crohane Lake at which, in spite of the map's assertion to the contrary, there is only a straggle of trees set back from the shore.

If you have plenty of time you might like to wander (or more accurately struggle - this is tough terrain) along the western shore of Crohane Lake. However the route proper continues to the col to the west, south of the highest Bennaunmore (454m). To avoid unnecessary climbing a bearing from the lake might be useful. At this col you may like to make a there-and-back to Bennaunmore - after all, it does give the route its title (the time is included in the walking time above). Then make a short, steep, tough descent westward through ancient oaks to the floor of Cappagh Glen. This is a lovely stretch: trees clothing the slopes on both sides of the narrow defile with the stern crags of Eskduff close by on the other side.

Turn right on the valley floor and follow the stream, keeping the main river on the left. This is a pleasant walk and an easy one, except for the occasional heaps of boulders to climb. Clamber through a narrow gap between cliffs into more open country. Continue to follow the stream until it swings decisively right. Here look out for a track a little higher up on the right on the lower slopes of Bennaunmore. Walk to it and follow it roughly north (it's indistinct in places) to cross a gate. Continue north on what is now a good track, the main stream still on the left, past an abandoned house and onto tarmac. The start is only a few hundred metres further on along the shore.

An Easy Variation: *An enjoyable stroll into the remote recesses of the Cappagh Glen. However the rocky peaks and cliffs of Bennaunmore and Eskduff tower closely above so don't expect wide panoramas.*

Drive onward from the parking place given for the main route for a short distance to park carefully at a fork in the track (that's all it is at this stage) where the right fork ends at a farmhouse.

Route: The comparatively high, rocky mountain facing you as you near the end of the drive and close to you at the parking place is Bennaunmore and the route is directly to the right (west) of this mountain. If you keep this in mind you will have no trouble finding your way into the Cappagh Glen. ■

ROUTE 28: KNOCKNADOBAR

Except for a few scenic corries on its northern side, Knocknadobar (690m) itself is a none too exciting mountain. However, its location close to Dingle Bay and a little aloof from the main mountains of Kerry means that the views from the length of the long, mostly gently-sloped ridge which culminates in the summit are superb, with the seaward views over cliff and island particularly impressive.

Getting There: From Cahersiveen (about 8 miles (13km) away) take the N70 towards Glenbeigh, turning left off it (signposted) to park at the carpark overlooking the beach at Kells (GR 556879). Take care that you choose the correct road to the beach as there are several misleading roads in this area. The start is also within easy reach of Glenbeigh. **Buses:** 279, 280 along the N70.

Walking Time: 5.25 hours (distance 15km, climb 760m). This may be shortened by parking your car somewhere on the road west of Kells, but in this area even road walks are enjoyable.

Difficulties: None.

Map: Sheet 83.

Route: From the carpark turn right (west) and walk the narrow road towards the village of Roads. After about 2km continue straight ahead at a junction on the right bearing a waymark, but only for a few hundred metres. Here, with a bit of luck (required because there seems to be the prospect of further houses along this road) you will find unrestricted access to open country on the left.

Climb steadily, veering slightly left of a direct upward assault to aim for an impressive viewpoint close to the western side of Roads Lough, which is set in a deep corrie with fearsome cliffs to its south and rocky crags to its east. Continue upward past the corrie to reach a boggy col between pts 612m and 633m.

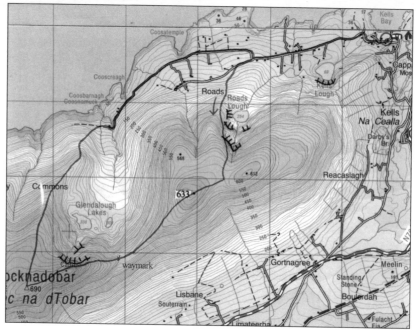

From here for some considerable time the underfoot conditions are firm, the slope is gentle and the views, which encompass a large part of Iveragh as well as the neighbouring Dingle peninsula are good. Climb the indistinct pt 633m, then descend to the col on the eastern side of Knocknadobar, which offers good views over cliffs on the right down onto the two lakes Glendalough. There is also a waymark here, a useful navigational aid. From here climb directly to the summit, where cliffs on the right gives enhanced views of the two lakes and much more besides. When you reach the summit cairn you may like to stroll a bit further to the large, solid cross.

Back at the cairn head north with a touch of east to reach a spur of high ground ending with a rocky and steep descent. Rather than clambering down directly you can veer left from the end of the spur to descend on grass. Where the slope eases head right to reach a track running parallel and close to the sea. This is a dramatic coastline viewed from a location high above it, with cliff, foaming surf and what looks strikingly like a cliff-bound island, though the map thinks otherwise.

Once on this track the rest is easy. Take it onward to reach its end at a tee. Turn left here and in no time at all you will be back at the start in Kells. ∎

ROUTE 29: MANGERTON

An over-long track leads to superb views over the Devil's Punch Bowl and down into the L-shaped Horses' Glen. Behind the rim of the Horses' Glen hides the boggy plateau of Mangerton (839m), so this is a route treading the narrow line between memorable terrain and dull.

Getting There: The start (at GR 983848) is about 5 miles (8km) from Killarney. From the town take the N71, turning left off it after about 2½ miles (4km) (signposted reassuringly 'Mangerton 2¾'). After 1 mile turn right (it's on a corner) also signposted for Mangerton. Drive onward for a little over a mile to park at or near a concrete bridge on the left. There is plenty of room for parking here.

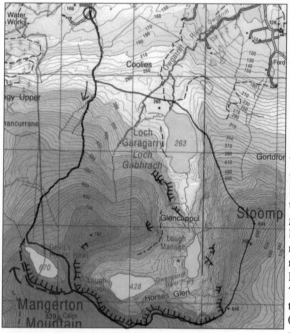

Walking Time: 5 hours (distance 14km, climb 780m). The extra time for a steep descent is offset by the initial track walking.

Difficulties: The steep descent from Stoompa and the last trek across bogland may prove tiring. Navigation is easy, though in bad weather it is advisable to avoid the summit of Mangerton, which adds little to the walk and makes the navigation more difficult.

Map: Sheets 78 and 79. "Killarney National Park" (1:25 000) covers the same area as 78.

Route: Cross the concrete bridge and take the rough track beyond all the way south to the Devil's Punch Bowl, a corrie lake. The track is easy enough to follow, being straight and relentlessly uphill for much of the way, though near the Bowl it veers right to traverse a shoulder.

The first sight of the lake (1.75 hours) is from a lovely location, a good spot for a break. You find yourself here high above the Bowl on the rocky moraine at its north-eastern side. Beyond it you will see the Mangerton plateau stretching away on the near horizon, with an obvious ramp leading to it rising from the lake's left. It is a short but steep climb to the plateau, the Bowl on the right and the Horses' Glen on the left. If the weather is clear and you are intent on bagging peaks you might like to cross the peat hags to reach the summit of Mangerton

(839m) 300m away. Mangerton's main interest is that it is the most uninteresting summit in Ireland: its only distinguishing feature is its trig pillar - and an arrow formed of stones indicating the way back. (You can't take it with you.)

Back at the plateau edge head roughly east, Lough Erhogh far below. This is a truly delightful stretch with the steep sides of the huge corrie immediately on the left. After 2km or so the cliff edge swings abruptly - and permanently - at right-angles north (don't mistake this swing for either of two abrupt but minor swings before it). Continue along the edge, Lough Managh now far below, to climb north to the flattish top of twinned-topped Stoompa (705m, 3.75 hours), the only distinct peak of the day.

From Stoompa continue north steeply downward to reach the shore of broad Lough Garagarry. Once there walk along the shore and cross the outlet stream on a neat bridge a hundred or so metres from the lake. From here you must reach the nearest point of the outward track about 1km away to the west by crossing very soggy bogland. Make sure you do not miss the track as it may not be too distinct at this point. Once on it turn right for the nearby start.

Short Variation: Take the main route on the dullish slog up to the Devil's Punch Bowl and continue on it to the edge of the Mangerton plateau. Then turn right to follow the cliff edge down the spur to the west of the Bowl and so regain the outward track. Walking time is 3.75 hours (distance 9km, climb 680m). ∎

ROUTE 30: MULLAGHANATTIN

A splendid high-level walk, much of it along a narrow ridge west of Mullaghanattin (773m) with superb views in all directions, and culminating at its sharp summit. After it the broader eastern end is a trifle dull underfoot but the views continue to be superb.

Getting There: A long and slow drive from any direction. From *Killarney* (23 miles (37km)) take the N71 and R568 (at Moll's Gap), turn right at the second of two close-together turns after about 6 miles (10km) from Moll's Gap (signposted Ballaghbeama Gap), continue straight ahead after 1.4 miles, where the main road swings right. Park (at GR 746746) at the turn left after another 1.9 miles.

From *Glencar* (12 miles (19km)) take the road initially west to turn left after about a half-mile and so cross Ballaghbeama Gap. Turn right about 3½ miles (6km) beyond the Gap. Park at the turn left after another 1.9 miles (3.1km). Make sure that you park carefully well off the road as bales of silage are sometimes moved along it and this takes up its full width - and more. Enquire locally if you are in doubt. **Bus:** 280 (summer only) along the R568.

Walking Time: 4.5 hours (distance 10km, climb 1000m).

Difficulties: A usually wet descent at the end, otherwise fairly good underfoot. Navigation is generally easy but in this remote area care is always essential. Note that there is a fence (or in a few places boundary stones) from north-west of the first summit pt 531m, all the way along the route to the col east of Mullaghanattin, except that veers south of this summit.

Map: Sheet 78. Most of the route is also covered on the 1:25 000 "Macgillycuddy's Reeks" map.

Route: Don't panic! The distinctive Matterhorn-like peak of Mullaghanattin is nowhere to be seen as you emerge from your car, but you are not (necessarily) at the wrong starting place. Perversely the summit can be seen clearly from almost anywhere except the start.

I have chosen a clockwise circuit because it is easier to cut the route short from the eastern side at the end of the day rather than via the slabby descent of the west. There may be factors which might dictate that you walk anti-clockwise. Either way the route directions will be equally intelligible.

Take the turn left (west) to the nearby first farm and ask permission here to go through the yard. The slabs of the first peak lie directly behind the farm and it is straight climb to the nearly level area around pt 531m, after which the climb resumes to pt 639m. The route from here on is pure joy: a narrow ridge, marvellous views and no navigational problems. After Beoun (752m) the route swings east over some rocky hummocks to face Mullaghanattin itself. Before the summit a small plaque commemorating a climber who died in an accident here may be some reassurance that you are on course (given its nature, maybe it won't be too reassuring in other respects).

The long climb to the summit ends at the trig pillar of Mullaghanattin (773m, 3.25 hours) and predictably excellent views. After it the one vital navigational point to remember is to swing right 1km from the summit (at pt 594m) and so face a broad

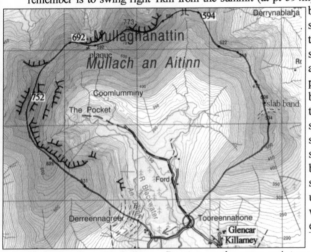

boggy spur running south. The only feature of note on this spur is the slab band across the route before pt 534m, in bad visibility an indication that you must swing south-west at the next summit to reach the start. The descent is boggy and steep, a slight anti-climax, but unlikely to impair what I hope was an enjoyable day.

Bad Weather Variation: *Starting at the same point as the main route this variation explores the valley directly south of Mullaghanattin, where great cliffs and steep grassy slopes rise in most directions. A comparatively gentle slope leads from here directly to the summit of Mullaghanattin, so you can extend this route greatly if you wish. If so walk west from the summit of Mullaghanattin for more dramatic scenery and better underfoot conditions.*

Walking Time: 1.5 hours (distance 5km, climb about 100m), but you might pleasurably spend some time wandering around here.

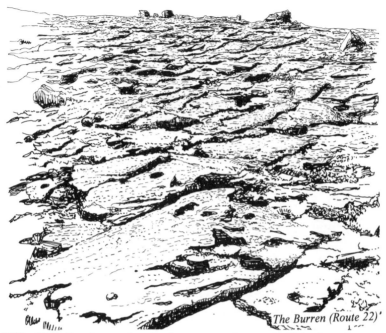

The Burren (Route 22)

Difficulties: Rough ground, and a river to cross that may be high after rain.
Map: Sheet 78, though it is hardly necessary.
Route: Continue onward (north) along the road, which shortly deteriorates to a track and bridgelessly leaves you to ford the river on the left unaided. Take the left fork after a few hundred metres (the right fork ends shortly at a ruin close to the river) and continue on it to its end at a substantial ruin sheltering close to a line of high ground.

Keep this house on the right and continue along the foot of the high ground to cross a stream. At this stage you are walking roughly west and following the main stream in the Pocket, as this area is called. There are still signs of fields about here down on the left but the main focus of attention is the formidable expanse of mountain rising near at hand described in the introduction. Specifically, you might note a huge flat-topped boulder ahead, which makes a convenient finishing point to the outward leg.

Rather than directly retrace your steps for the return you might like to take to the crest of the high ground, which gives good views on both sides. You will thereby cross a modest defile where a stream has cut through the high ground and continue along it to resume the outward walk somewhere around the substantial ruin noted above. Keep on the track from here back to the start. ■

A most impressive steep climb around rocky slabs to the summit of Hungry Hill.
The descent is over undistinguished Derryclancy and then to two lakes lying
precariously between lines of bare, rocky cliffs. A walk in wild and dramatic
surroundings.

Getting There: From Glengarriff take the R572 past the junction of the Healy
Pass Road in Adrigole. Less than a mile from this junction, pass a sign on the
right for the waterfall, cross a bridge and immediately turn right. Drive for a
further mile and park on waste ground on the right (GR 783493).

Walking Time: 4.75 hours
(distance 10km, climb 800m)
including a half-hour over
Naismith to avoid slabs on the
initial ascent and 15 minutes
for slabs on the descent from
Hungry Hill.

Difficulties: The summit plateau of Hungry Hill is not the
place to be in bad visibility, as
the cliffs and slabs surrounding
it are most intimidating. Keep
this walk for a clear day.

Map: Sheet 84.

Route: Walk onward along the
road, shortly crossing a stile on
the left leading into boggy country. Head upward and south-westward, evading
further up the odd harmless outcrop. As you climb the valley where you started
opens out to reveal fields and the occasional tree. That slender waterfall, incidentally, zig-zagging into the valley, issues from Coomarkane Lake, and is the
way to go if you are on the variation.

At length you will reach the brow of the hill, perhaps at old turf workings.
Here the view to the south opens out over Bear Island snuggling in at the side of
Bantry Bay. All very pleasant, but as you walk west along the crest your gaze
will more likely turn towards the intimidating horizontal lines of slabs, one
above the other, seemingly to the very summit of Hungry Hill. If like me, you
are a person of a nervous disposition, you will not wish to tackle these slabs directly. Instead veer to the left to evade each unclimbable line, of which there are
more than several. You will therefore find yourself eventually above Park Lough
(by which a road runs) and climbing roughly north. On this course you will
climb to a tiny flat area (at GR 764490) and be cheered to know that nearly all
the slabs and most of the climbing to the summit are behind. In fact the well-
constructed cairn near the south summit is only 100m climbing away.

Once on the south summit, navigation is easy and the ground though a little
soggy, allows easy walking. Walk to the trig pillar marking the highest point

(685m), where you may be led to wonder if any mountain anywhere has a tamer summit compared to its ferocious flanks.

The descent to the col facing Derryclancy requires some care. Walk north to the small cairn marking the north summit. From here, don't walk directly towards the col as this would take you over some horrific slabs; instead head about north-west for a few hundred metres, and then swing east, a route which admittedly makes navigation more difficult.

At the boggy col you can admire Coomadayallig Lake down on the right below lines of slabs. Don't attempt a direct descent as it will bring you over heartbreakingly difficult slabs. Instead climb through soft ground to the summit of Derryclancy (554m), a quite mundane affair with outcrops and a small lake, the only one directly on the route so far, and so maybe some help in navigation.

The idea now is to reach the eastern side of Coomadayallig Lake, specifically the small, narrow peninsula on that side. If slabs threaten on this descent head slightly (not too far!) to the left of a direct bearing. The lake is in a magnificent location, with great cliffs guarding the eastern side of Hungry Hill rising on its (the lake's) far side. Walk to the southern tip of the lake where another compass bearing might be no harm to reach Coomarkane Lake to the south. This lake is less than a kilometre away but the gradients, a sharp climb followed by an equally sharp and longer descent, is of no help in finding it. What a location! It is even better than Coomadayallig's with great bare cliffs to the right, wild and rough rocky ground in other directions and the lake itself occupying a hollow in a narrow strip of boggy ground.

Follow the outlet stream down for a few hundred metres, or at least keep in touch with it since in places it runs as a waterfall between steeply rising slabs. Below this steep ground leave the waterfall so that it is down on the left and head for the stile near where you started. Once across turn right for the nearby start.

Short Variations: Walk to Coomarkane (1.5 hours, total there and back) or Coomadayallig Lake (2.25 hours) using the start of the main route. ■

ROUTE 32: CUMMEENGEERA

A dramatic terrain of highly contorted rock strata makes for hard going to start, after which is a high-level walk along the edge of cliffs and steep slopes with magnificent views down into the head of the remote valley of Cummeengeera.

Getting There: The start is about 17 miles (27km) south-west of Kenmare. Take the R571 to Lauragh (GR 7758). Still on the R571, continue straight ahead through the scattered village, turning left at the sign 'Glanmore Lake'. Take the first right after 0.6 miles and park after another 0.9 miles around the junction on the left (GR 763560). Parking is hard to find on the narrow road and you may have to search around if your party has more than 2 or 3 cars. **Bus:** 282 to near Lauragh on the R571.

Walking Time: 6 hours (distance 12km, climb 1080m) including 0.75 hours over Naismith for route finding and difficult terrain near the start and 0.25 hours for a fairly steep descent near the end.

Difficulties: Slabs to negotiate at the start; otherwise the terrain is fairly good. Navigation is quite easy in good weather except for the section between the first summit, Cummeenahillan, and the trig pillar on Coomacloghane; this is likely to be a nightmare of indistinct 'summits' in bad visibility. The variation below avoids this section. Be wary about descending into Cummeengeera in the first half of the route as there are extensive sections of difficult slabs close to the valley floor that not marked on the map. If you can, keep going to make an easy descent after Bireca (see below).

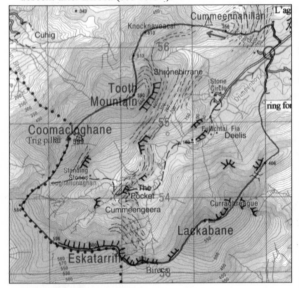

Map: Sheet 84.

Route: From the junction around which you parked, walk back the way you came to the first bungalow, now on the left. Just beyond it take the gated driveway uphill, cross another gate and just before the only farmhouse on this driveway turn left into open country.

The first task is to climb Cummeennahillan. Here the problem, apart from evading gorse and ferns, is to avoid being driven leftward by the lie of the rock strata; you will probably have to cross slabs to keep on course. Cummeenahillan (356m) is a magnificent viewpoint, particularly towards the highly contorted strata of the route ahead. It has no definite summit marker but the boggy plain just to its west is sufficient evidence in retrospect that you have climbed it.

The next target is Knocknaveachal. As indicated above it is a navigator's nightmare, an area of rocky outcrops, slabs and grassy ramps and with two notional summits both of 513m, with a distinct swing from west to south-west to get from one to the other. Not that the approach to the next mountain, Tooth is much better. There is an easily avoidable, long, almost vertical slab on the way to Tooth, or at least there is on some approaches so don't be surprised if you don't find it. The summit (590m) is marked by a jumble of puddles and rocky outcrops and so is almost impossible to identify exactly. However, after it the terrain is much easier, with outcrops and soft ground and this transition may be some help in extremis.

Coomacloghane (599m), the next mountain to be climbed, is more accommodating. Though this 'peak' barely rises above the surrounding bogland, it does have a trig pillar, a most useful landmark. From here on walk south-west for over a kilometre to reach the grassy plateau marking the high ground on the south-west side of Cummeengeera.

Having attained this plateau at Motidhu (584m) the rule is to keep cliffs and steep ground on the left, walking south-east at first and then swinging left to take in the undistinguished Eskatarriff (over 640m) and then the small but steep-sided rocky pinnacle of Bireca (531m), an excellent landmark. From about here on the views down into Cummeengeera are magnificent, considerably better than those from the opposite side of the valley. You should be able to see a tiny deserted village down in the valley, sheltering under stern slabs and cliffs. At the low point just beyond Bireca you can easily escape into the valley, though considering the walk ahead, I hope this isn't necessary.

Continuing along the high ground beyond this escape point there is a short but stiff climb to Lackabane (602m) and hardly any climb to its sister peak, Curraghreague (over 590m), which has high cliffs on its north-west side that drop in long columns into the glen far below. This may be a useful reassurance point since the descent is nigh.

But not that nigh. The route runs north-east from Curraghreague to a col from which it looks as if there is an easy descent to the start. Not so. This direct approach is an area of hidden rocks and high vegetation so it is necessary to climb about 30m to the next hill, pt 406m. From here descend north-east to a level grassy area and then make what will probably prove to be a tedious descent to a prominent ring fort visible from a great distance. At the ring fort take a path northwards, which shortly becomes a narrow track, and then a wider track. Cross the Drimminboy River on it to reach the nearby start.

Much Easier Variation: Drive onward from the parking place mentioned above to park at the end of tarmac (GR 754553). Take the road onward, which later becomes a track, to cross the main stream in the valley. Then climb on an intermittent path, keeping crags on the right, into the upper valley. At its end you will reach the remains of a village sheltering under a huge slab of sandstone. An awesome spot. Walking time (one way) is about an hour. From here you can return by the same route or try .....

An 'Easier' Variation: Easier in that it avoids the navigationally difficult terrain at the start of the main route. However, it does include some hard clambering over rocks along a semi-waterfall, which you might not enjoy. *Do not attempt this variation in the reverse direction.*

From the most remote ruin in the deserted village climb by the stream directly behind the house. If it's any consolation the first part of this climb is the hardest. When you emerge onto comparatively level ground, you can turn right to cross another gully containing a stream and then walk across easy ground to Loughanunaghan to the north-west. From here walk either to the col to the west or, if you require further assurance, to the trig pillar on Coomacloghane. You can pick up the main route from either point. ■

ROUTE 33: COOMASAHARN

A steep initial climb ends in a gentle walk with moorland on one side and a line of magnificent corries on the other, that holding Coomasaharn Lake being particularly impressive. The peaks themselves, of which Coomacarrea (772m) is the highest, are undistinguished. Two possible descents, one by a narrow but safe path along an arête between two of the corries, are given below.

Getting There: From *Killarney*, 26 miles (42km) to the east, drive through Killorglin, here taking the N70 to Glenbeigh. In Glenbeigh fork left at the Towers Hotel and continue for 4.4 miles (7.1km) to a sharp bend to the right (GR 636852). There is parking for a few cars at a deserted house on the right just before this bend. From *Cahirsiveen* (16 miles (26km)) take the N70 and after it passes under a bridge (at GR 6289) take the second turn right, turn right at the tee and drive straight ahead to the start. **Buses:** 279 or 280 (summer only) along the N70. If travelling by bus you can modify the walk to start and/or end at Mountain Stage (GR 6289) or the junction just to its east.

Walking Time: 6 hours (distance 16km, climb 940m) including a little time over Naismith for the steep descent.

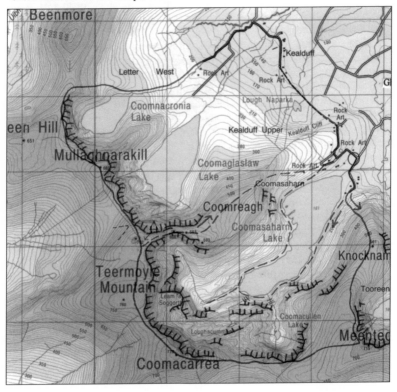

Difficulties: With unmistakable cliffs almost everywhere close at hand, navigation is easy. Underfoot conditions, though boggy for much of the route are not so bad as to cause delays.

Map: Sheet 83.

Route: From the bend, take the track across a nearby bridge and choose any convenient place beyond it to turn left off it and climb steeply through rocky outcrops to Knocknaman (561m), a shoulder rather than a summit.

Now on comparatively gently rising ground head south, keeping initially to the crest of the spur. Then gradually veer left off it to climb Meenteog (715m) from where you can study the fine corrie to its north. (In bad conditions don't risk this detour to Meenteog; simply keep steep ground on the right after Knocknaman.)

Walk west from Meenteog to the cliffs overlooking Coomasaharn Lake. Once at these cliffs you can relax. Navigation is simple - keep the cliffs on the right - and the views magnificent. Apart from a whole range of mountains, the huge corrie around Coomasaharn Lake is at your feet, a corrie with at least two other lakes sheltering in ledges among the cliffs. Later on, take a look at the jagged cliff edge, Leam a Soggorth, running at right angles to the main line of the cliffs.

But we are ahead of ourselves. From the low point west of Meenteog, climb sharply to Coomacarrea (772m), the highest point of the day, from where the cliffs swing gradually right. Teermoyle (760m, 3.25 hours), an indistinct summit, is reached after a gentle drop from Coomacarrea followed by a slight rise.

From Teermoyle descend north to a large expanse of pebbles and soft ground around pt 702m. If you want to do the short variation (it reduces the walking time by 1.75 hours) turn east here to descend a grassy slope and so reach a narrow arête with a path winding along its top, beyond which is a rough triangle of grassy ground. From this ground descend roughly north-east to the road system near the start.

If you want the main route, continue from Teermoyle with the cliffs on the right, passing a vee of track on the left and a good indication of your position, especially useful if you intended only the short variation. Pass the corrie holding Coomaglaslaw Lake, a pale imitation of the corrie passed earlier, and climb Mullaghnarkill (665m), crowned by large slabs of rock.

You cannot reach lower ground directly north-east from Mullaghnarkill. Instead contour round the eastern side of Been Hill (no need to climb it) and when the cliffs on the right ease, swing east over rough ground to reach the outlet stream from Coomnacronia Lake.

The rest is an easy 5km, mostly on track or path through upland bog and fields. Start by keeping the stream on the right until you meet a track, follow it across the stream (alas, no bridge) and continue down to tarmac, turning right here away from a bridge and a house. Walk to the end of the road and along its continuation as a track, closing gates carefully as you advance.

After you pass Lough Naparka the track rises sharply and bends to the right to reach a fork at a deserted house (the map confusingly shows this section of track as a road). Turn left here, left again onto the nearby road and left yet again to reach the nearby start.

Lakeshore Variation: *Starting at the same point as the main route, this is a short walk but not an easy one, with difficult clambering around lakeshore crags. The eastern shore of Coomasaharn Lake is tough but rewarding territory, encompassing spectacular nearby views of waterfalls and towering cliffs. If you want to make life easy but unexciting, walk the western shore only.*

Walking Time: In theory this is a walk of 4km with practically no climbing and so should take an hour. You might do it in that time if you walk a there-and-back along the western shore. However you could easily spend 3 hours or more if you want to do the entire route and so explore the area fully.

Difficulties: Some crags that are quite difficult to negotiate after rain.

Map: Sheet 78 or 83 though hardly needed.

Route: Take the track from the parking place to cross the nearby bridge and continue along it until it ends. Here take an intermittent path past a small peninsula. Soon after follow a distinct path by the lakeshore.

The difficult part now looms. At lakeshore level pass below the cascades of the stream pouring down from Coomacullen Lake and then keep about 10-15m above the shore, picking your way between crags and steep grassy slopes until you are across a second cascade, that from Loughacummeen.

From here on it is easy to keep to the lakeshore. However rather than marching directly back, why not follow the third stream into its valley, climbing the several steps over which the stream plunges and admiring the mighty cliffs which abruptly terminate the eastern side of Termoyle Mountain.

That done, keep the lakeshore on the right to pass a dome-shaped rocky promontory and a small wooded island, before crossing rough fields to meet a gate. Take the grassy track beyond to the initial track of the day and walk the short distance to the start. ■

ROUTE 34: GOUGANE BARRA

A scenic lake featuring a tiny church on a minute peninsula with woods, rugged mountains and cliffs penning it in on most sides, Gougane Barra is a trifle chocolate-boxy. This route gives good views with rocky terrain on the first, southern leg and much boggier on the northern one.

Getting There: The start is 20 miles (32km) west of Macroom and also 20 miles east of Glengarriff. From *Macroom* take the N22 *east* for a short distance, here turn right onto the R584, turn right to Gougane Barra (well signposted) after passing through Ballingeary. From *Glengarriff* take the N71 towards Bantry, branch left onto the R584, drive through the Pass of Keimaneigh and turn left shortly after. Park around the church (GR 092659). **Bus:** 255 to Gougane Barra.

Walking Time: 4.5 hours (distance 13km, climb 580m).

Difficulties: The boggy ground has been mentioned. Navigation is quite demanding in bad visibility. There are a number of small landmarks on the route but if you lose them you could find yourself in quite featureless terrain with your route to lower ground blocked by small, irregular but none-theless impassable cliffs and crags.

Map: Sheet 85.

Route: From the church walk onward taking the first turn left beside toilets modelled, for reasons unknown to me, on an African hut. Keep to this track for about 10 minutes by which time you will have passed a small field on the right and the track is heading east and disobligingly downhill. Leave it here and head uphill and south-west heading towards Foilastookeen, which is far from a distinct peak, though impressive cliffs fall on its north-west side. The first landmark lies ahead: a fence corner beyond Foilastookeen. Follow the branch running roughly west to pass a small lake (unnamed on the map), a larger lake,

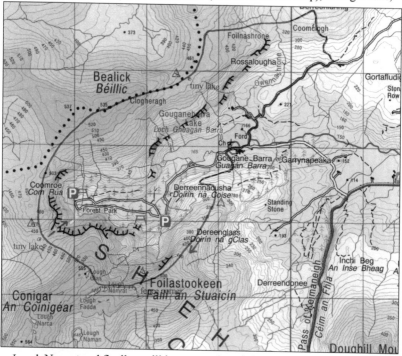

Lough Namrat and finally a still larger one, Lough Fadda.

At Lough Fadda the fence ends so a compass bearing is necessary to find Lough Glas perched close by on the plateau to the north-west. From about here the mighty line of the Reeks to the west is prominent and, much nearer, the imposing Caoinkeen cliffs. Rocks disappear for a while as you push north-west from Lough Glas, aiming for a tiny circular lake at a distinct low point. Just before it you will cross a fence (use the stile here) and, at 2 hours into the walk, you can decide whether to go on or retreat - and let's face it you have walked the more interesting half of the route. If homeward bound take the deep gully on the right after crossing the stile; this will take you to the valley floor and a road. If you want to go on head north into slabs, pass the indistinct pt 503m and then head north-east over boggy ground to reach the more easterly of the two 'summits' of Bealick (535m), distinguished only because it has an obvious cairn, the only one on the route.

From Bealick head for another tiny circular lake to the north-east, passing through boggy country though with a few mighty slabs to add a bit of colour. This lake, a trifle nondescript though it is, is the key to the next leg, a contorted one designed to avoid cliffs to its east and north-east.

Walk north from the lake across bogland for about 10 minutes until faced by rockier rising ground. Turn east here to descend by a pleasant stream, a tributary of the Owennashrone River, or a little imaginatively perhaps, a source of the River Lee. Cross a soggy, tussocky area where several such tributaries are gathering, the idea here being to reach a track heading uphill on the far side. Once on the track, simply follow it down to tarmac, turn right here to take a meandering course through upland fields. At the bottom of this road, and now you are close to Gougane Barra Lake, turn left and right for the nearby start. ■

Gougane Barra (Route 34)